50 URGENT THINGS YOU NEED TO DO BEFORE THE MILLENNIUM

50 URGENT THINGS YOU NEED TO DO BEFORE THE MILLENNIUM

PROTECT YOURSELF, YOUR FAMILY, AND YOUR FINANCES FROM THE UPCOMING COMPUTER CRISIS!

WILLIAM D. McGUIRE

A Lynn Sonberg Book

WARNER BOOKS

A Time Warner Company

Warner Books, Inc., 1271 Avenue of the Americas, New York, NY 10020
Visit our Web site at www.warnerbooks.com

W A Time Warner Company

Printed in the United States of America
First Warner Books Printing: August 1999

10 9 8 7 6 5 4 3 2 1

Library of Congress Cataloging-in-Publication Data

McGuire, William D.
    50 urgent things you need to do before the millennium : protect yourself, your family, and your finances from the upcoming computer crisis! / William D. McGuire
        p.   cm.
    ISBN 0-446-67566-0
    1. Year 2000 date conversion (Computer systems) 2. Home economics.
    I. Title. II. Title: Fifty urgent things you need to do before the millennium.
QA76.76.S64M39   1999
005.1'6—dc21   99-24076
                                                        CIP

Book design by Nancy Sabato

TO MY WIFE, LYNN. AND TO MORIAH, AUSTIN, AND JONATHAN,

INHERITORS OF THE TWENTY-FIRST CENTURY.

CONTENTS

DEALING WITH UNCLE SAM AND THE LAW   109

KEEPING UP TO DATE   119

THE LAST WORD   137

INTRODUCTION: Y2K 101

Y2K seems like such a terribly simple problem that it's easy to dismiss. Unless they're reprogrammed, many computers will stop working at the stroke of midnight, December 31, 1999, because they can't recognize the "00" date field. Since this is a well-known fact, the people in charge of computers will simply go ahead and fix them before that time, right?

In reality, Y2K (for Year 2 Kilos, or thousands) is anything but simple. Millions of computerized machines with billions of microchips are involved; and the total cost of the whole business, from fixing those machines to cleaning up after the ones that fail, could add up to over a trillion dollars.

In the United States, the experts say that nearly all the computers will be corrected in time. Unfortunately, that may not be good enough to avert disaster. The small percentage of computers and other devices that aren't fixed—perhaps less than 10 percent of all machines—have the potential to wreak havoc on our lives and the world economy. Power and water could stop flowing, airplanes may no longer fly, traffic lights will wink out.

In the coming months you'll no doubt be hearing from a merry band of experts and prophets who will be predicting vastly different scenarios, ranging from the end of civilization to just a minor bump in the road, of what will occur as a result of Year 2000 computer problems. But nobody really knows what Y2K will bring—and nobody can know.

The best we can do is make educated guesses and prepare for the worst. If the worst doesn't happen, then our preparations will have been for naught. But look at it this way: It's smart to take precautions. We wear seat belts and lock our doors at night, but we don't gripe about the bother if our car never crashes or a burglar doesn't so much as glance toward our home.

Approximately 90 percent of all computer software and 80 percent of all automated machines being used in the world today may be affected. "The list of possible disruptions adds up to a mighty ugly scenario," says Edward Yardeni, chief economist at Deutsche Bank, who predicts a 40 percent chance of a world-wide recession due to Y2K problems. "This could affect the world well into the next century."

So how did we get into this jam? The answer to that question can be traced to the dawn of the computer age. Back in the 1950s and 1960s, computer memory was ruinously expensive, costing about ten thousand times more than it does today. A five-million-dollar UNIVAC computer from the 1950s didn't possess the computing power or data-storage memory that a seven-hundred-dollar PC has today.

So to save precious memory space, computer programmers cut corners wherever they could, especially in parts of the pro-gramming code—the instructions that make a computer oper-ate—that came up again and again, like date fields.

So the year 1967 was shortened to 67, and so on. No one at the time gave this convention a second thought. After all, the turn of the century seemed impossibly far away, as many of us who remember the 1950s and 1960s can attest.

As the years went by, the two-digit convention stuck, because new software programs had to work with the previous generation of computers, which all used this two-digit format. Unlike personal computers, which didn't even exist back when all this started, large corporate computer systems cost millions of dollars and were generally kept in place and expanded with additional memory dedicated to still more tasks. Plenty of corporate and government computers that were built twenty or thirty years ago are still in service today—with lots of updates and additions, of course.

Without expensive reprogramming, these so-called legacy computer systems will hum along until the last day of 1999, when at midnight, the date will change from 1999 to 2000. Then, according to the way such computers "think," 99 + 1 = 00, and the machine assumes that 00 is 1900, not 2000. Some computers may simply stop operating when presented with dates that go against internal rules. Or they may begin making horrible mistakes, like adding interest to your loan dating back ninety-nine years instead of one, or rejecting perfectly good perishable inventory on the incorrect assumption that it's more than one hundred years old.

At this point you might legitimately ask what's so hard about fixing a couple of silly digits. Send in the programmers to make these computers either accept the two extra digits or navigate around the problem. Surely, some may believe, Bill Gates and his crew at Microsoft will introduce Y2K 1.0, the all-purpose cure for the bug. But that's never going to happen. Here's why. At least six hundred different computer languages—the format in which individual lines of computer code are written—are in use in the world today. A typical mid-range business computer system may have several million lines of code, written in perhaps a half-dozen programming languages by dozens, sometimes hundreds, of different programmers.

To make matters more complicated, many of the computer systems like the ones that run banks or payroll functions are put together in a modular style. That is, one segment might be written in COBOL and another in C++. So the Y2K fix for the COBOL portion won't carry over to the C++ without rewriting that section of the code and so on.

Fixing each section of the code is not a straightforward process either. The earlier computer programmers didn't adhere to fixed rules. They often wrote code in their own style, using obscure conventions. When programmers today take apart that code—and it's hard to find programmers who know some of these languages anymore—like a three-million-page book with no index, they find lots of lines that don't make sense without extensive and costly investigation.

The cost to reprogram the world's computers is hard to estimate with much accuracy, but the technology consultants Gartner Group say it will be in the neighborhood of $1 trillion. That doesn't include all the lawsuits that could result from Y2K glitches. The Giga Information Group reckons the total value of those suits could top $1 trillion, making Y2K the biggest litigation event ever.

The Y2K error is built into everything from Microsoft Windows 95 to the wiring and microchips used in home appliances, on farms, and in factories—billions of chips, all told.

•   •   •

In today's digital world, where so many computers are interconnected, one bad circuit can spoil the whole bunch. For example, in 1998 the cell phone and pager network for a large section of the nation went down because one chip in one satellite failed to do its job. In 1997, many small businesses were crippled after just one parcel service, UPS, went on strike. Now consider how disruptive it might be to the U.S. economy if even a few vital services are stopped or curtailed by Y2K computer failures.

The bug affects much more than computers. The microchip has found its way into countless devices, from watches to toasters to VCRs. These so-called embedded microchips are wired into millions of devices, and they don't have computer code that can be rewritten. Instead, these chips must be either replaced, routed around, or tricked in some way to allow the devices they govern to continue to run.

The surprising truth is that although many machines, from household appliances to factory robots, perform functions seemingly unrelated to the date, they actually contain a hidden date calendar. That's because most microchips are not custom designed for a particular task. They're multipurpose, made to be sewn into the innards of a variety of machines. So the date function is there even if installed in a machine that has no need to track dates. Most of these machines, from milking equipment on farms to home security systems, will probably keep running after January 1, 2000; some of them will not, and there's little way, at this point, to tell which will and which won't.

Estimates for the number of devices with these embedded chips range up to 100 billion. In 1996 alone, more than seven billion embedded chips were shipped. So even if just a tiny percentage of these fail, that could affect millions of devices.

Look around your household and you'll probably discover you've got lots of devices with microchips. I did just that and was surprised by what I found: My VCR won't accept dates after 1999, and my laptop computer shut down when I tried to enter 2000 into the date field. My expensive camcorder, purchased in 1996, doesn't understand 2000. I've got twenty or thirty other devices in my home that certainly have microchips, and I have no way of knowing whether they will be affected by Y2K or not.

That includes my 1992 Ford Taurus, three utility meters (electric, gas, and water), a satellite television system bought in 1995, a monitored burglar and fire alarm system, and a dozen or so software programs for my desktop computer (a Macintosh, which has always been Y2K compliant).

By multiplying my possible problems—and there are yet those I can't possibly discern—by most homes in the U.S. and millions of businesses, you can appreciate the extent of what we're dealing with. In Honolulu, for example, when the electric company decided to run a Y2K test, the entire power grid simply stopped working. The automakers in Detroit began work in 1997 to fix their Y2K systems, and it's not at all certain they'll be finished in time.

Thousands of small businesses and factories don't have the manpower to address the problem; they plan to "wing it" when the calendar odometer trips to 2000.

•   •   •

Your life may be affected by Y2K in ways you might not have considered. Your electricity might be interrupted, stores may not be able to get their food deliveries, mail could be slowed; your financial and personal records could disappear or become inaccessible. There might be long waits to get prescriptions filled because computer systems that connect health insurers may be down. Scanners, cash registers, and billing systems could simply stop working. What if you can't get cash from your ATM? Could your safety be endangered if the air-traffic control computers go haywire?

The federal government admits that despite increasingly frantic efforts, there's no guarantee that all of its computers will be Y2K compliant. The ramifications could be great if the government's computers malfunction, from missed Social Security checks to Internal Revenue Service snafus. Imagine the IRS computers running amok, spitting out absurd messages to taxpayers. (Okay, that's not so hard to imagine.)

Unpleasant possibilities all, but consider this: The Russians, along with half the world's countries, won't have made a dent in the Y2K problem by the time the new year dawns. What about nuclear missiles with 1960s and 1970s technology deep within Russia's underground bunkers? Or the machines that monitor security of Russia's airspace and at its weapons sites?

Perhaps as many as two-thirds of all the countries on earth are doing little or nothing to prepare for Y2K. They don't have the resources to even begin to battle the problem. This could lead to serious upset in worldwide commerce, pulling down all the economies of the world, even those that have licked their own Y2K computer bugs.

From cars to traffic to automated teller machines, our lives for better or worse are defined by the computer. Whether we wake up to chaos January 1, 2000, and begin a slide into social and economic unrest is largely a die that has already been cast. Nothing that can be done in the months leading up to the '00s will make much difference in the outcome, given how great the scope of the problem.

The betting money, and my own basically optimistic outlook, is on the side of reason and a measured approach to solving whatever foul-ups will occur. Mankind has shown a remarkable capacity to overcome all sorts of problems and Y2K isn't the first to come along, though it may well be one of the most complex.

I'm not a computer expert, but I've devoted much of my

career as a journalist over the past two decades to helping consumers make sense of their increasingly complicated financial and technological lives. Computers and microchips have brought us countless toys, conveniences, and life-saving devices. But they don't define our lives any more than the locomotive defined life in the 1880s, or the automobile in the 1920s.

What defines us is how we use these tools for the greater good, how we cope with adversity, and how we meet a challenge. This book, then, is about meeting the Y2K computer challenge: understanding the possible impact, preparing for it, and perhaps using it to our advantage to help build a more meaningful, less acquisitive, more sustainable life in the next century.

The following fifty chapters are a road map to coping with the probable effects of Y2K. Since the Y2K bug is like a hurricane waiting offshore, some of the precautions described here, such as stockpiling food and water, may seem foolish if the bug, like many hurricanes, veers away from the mainland and out to sea. Let your own good sense be the guide to how much you prepare.

STAY SAFE AND HEALTHY

1 CHECK UP ON NUCLEAR POWER

Background

Nuclear power plants are some of the most complicated computerized systems on earth. Built and designed back in the 1960s and 1970s, they typically employ hundreds of interrelated computers, many using program languages that have long since slipped into obscurity.

Over the past two decades, N-plants have compiled a sorry history of accidents and incompetence. Plants too numerous to mention have been ordered closed because of poor management and blunders that have come dangerously close to disaster.

Y2K is a challenge for nuclear operators. State and federal regulators have little legal authority and few resources to force Y2K compliance. Instead, all they can do is prod and urge nuclear operators to repair their potential Y2K computer problems. Only a handful of state commissions have issued rules requiring companies with nuclear power plants to even spell out their computer-testing plans. Meanwhile, the Nuclear Regulatory Commission (NRC), which oversees all the plants, won't comment on what any particular one is doing to comply, or whether they'll be ready for safe operation come January 1, 2000.

What You Can Do

If you live within one hundred miles of a nuclear power station, or even several hundred miles downwind of one, the industry's blanket assurances that Y2K will be solved in time simply won't suffice.

Call your state and local elected officials to insist that the nuclear plants in your area go off-line during the December 31, 1999–January 1, 2000, period. Already several electric utilities have quietly made plans to take their plants off-line during that period.

Find out whether the plant in your area is on the NRC's watch list, a public rating system used to classify plants on the basis of past and present operating problems.

Those who live within a few miles of a nuclear plant should obtain the drug potassium iodide, which the NRC plans to distribute to states with nuclear power plants. That drug can block a type of radiation that causes thyroid cancer. It's not a cure-all for radioactivity from a nuclear-power accident. It blocks only one of many isotopes—radioactive iodine—that may be emitted from a leak or meltdown. Still, without the drug, radioactive iodine is absorbed into the thyroid, where it can lead to thyroid cancer and other thyroid disorders.

A 130-milligram pill of potassium iodide can prevent radioactive iodine from entering the thyroid for several days, if taken within a few hours of exposure.

Residents near "troubled" nuclear plants, those Category 2 or Category 3 on the NRC watch list, should consider getting out of town for the holidays if the plant operator insists on staying online during the Y2K transition.

Finally, get a copy of the evacuation plan that's specific to your area; every nuclear plant is required by law to create such a plan and distribute it. You can obtain one by writing to the utility that operates the plant, or from the Nuclear Regulatory Commission.

RESOURCES

■ The NRC's Web site at http://nrc.gov has an up-to-date watch list. (Categories 2 and 3 are for plants that are under special watch for operating problems or that have been shut down.) The site also has nuclear safety and evacuation information.

■ The Federal Emergency Management Agency's Web site at http://fema.gov maintains a comprehensive databank about preparing for a nuclear plant mishap and what to do if there is an actual emergency.

■ The consumer group Public Citizen, through its Critical Mass Energy Project, monitors and reports on the nuclear power industry. You can contact one of the group's many local chapters, listed in the yellow pages, or online at http://www.citizen. org/cmep.

SECURE YOUR HOME | 2

BACKGROUND

Year 2000 computer problems could affect your home security in more ways than you might have considered. Security systems may fail. And there's the possibility that increased crime will occur during power outages or periods when law enforcement officials are overwhelmed and communications are down.

Better home security systems depend primarily on two things: power, and a live telephone connection. But they also depend on a prompt response from police, who may be quite busy this holiday season. Of course, this assumes that your system is working and has not gone haywire due to some Y2K glitch. We asked ADT, one of the largest makers of home security systems, about whether its systems are Y2K compliant. The company's answer was that there are no problems with its current systems. How about older security systems? Probably not, but we can't be sure, was the answer.

WHAT YOU CAN DO

If you've got a home security system that's wired to a central monitoring station, call the company that installed it to ask about Y2K compliance. If you can't find that company, look on the main box for the system, which is probably in a closet or in your basement, for the name of the manufacturer. If that fails, call the company that monitors the system for advice.

While you're at it, now's a good time to review your home security. Are your locks adequate? Can you escape from your home by more than one entrance? Where will family members gather in an emergency?

How would you respond if an intruder got into your home? That's a tough question for which there is no easy answer.

In some areas, it's becoming more common for intruders to barge through unlocked doors into households, often during the daytime hours. If you're like most people, you probably don't bother to lock your doors during the day; that could be a tragic mistake.

How about guns for protection? More and more people are deciding that guns are not the answer to their security problems. Back in 1973, nearly half of all households kept a gun. Now that number is down to less than a third. Handgun Control, Inc., puts it bluntly: "Bringing a handgun into the house is not a protective act. You're only putting your family at risk."

If you feel you must get a gun, take these steps: Get training in proper use of the weapon. Buy and use a trigger lock. Keep the gun and ammunition in separate places and under lock and key.

One more thing: What would you do if you needed help but picked up the phone and couldn't get through? One thing you might consider is a citizens band radio. By hooking it up to your TV antenna, you would be able to phone for help on channel 19, which is monitored by police departments all over the country. You may also want to consider a handheld or car battery–powered CB radio.

CHECK UP ON DOCTORS AND HOSPITALS

3

BACKGROUND

The average medium-size hospital has thirty thousand or so devices with microchips, and about one in six of these is susceptible to Y2K. Certain kinds of biomedical equipment, including patient-monitoring devices, CAT scanners, EKGs, IV drip machines, lab equipment, X-ray machines, and breathing machines could be affected. For example, IV drip machines controlled by a timer might not turn on. Automated inventory systems could reject blood and other perishables as being one hundred years old.

Midway through 1998, a survey of hospital administrators found that 69 percent think the health-care industry is poorly prepared to deal with Y2K. Patient billing and insurance records at hospitals or HMOs are vulnerable to Y2K as well. Although hospitals will be playing catch-up right up until the new year and beyond, experts say a small minority will not be ready in time.

The good news is there's no need to worry about implanted devices like pacemakers; they have no date functions. Still, a report from a prominent consultant to the industry starkly concludes that Y2K glitches "have significant potential to create errors that lead to unnecessary deaths in health care."

WHAT YOU CAN DO

Y2K probably won't be a crippling blow to health-care providers. Nearly every hospital in America has backup power generators, so even if power is disrupted, they'll keep functioning. And hospitals are always first to have their service restored after an outage.

The most important thing you can do to sidestep potential problems is to avoid elective surgery from mid-December until at least mid-January 2000. If there's any way you can put off a hospital stay during this time, do so.

If your condition doesn't permit this much flexibility, at the very least don't check into a hospital December 31 to January 1, unless of course you have a life-threatening emergency.

If you find yourself in the hospital during this crucial time period, don't be shy about asking questions of your doctor and the hospital staff: What machines will be used for my care during my stay? Have they been checked for Y2K compliance?

Since patient records and billing matters could also be affected, keep in close touch with your insurer and take careful notes of who you talked to and when, and what approvals were given. Ask for written confirmation of any verbal approvals or instructions.

If you are scheduled for a procedure, ask your physicians if you can hand-carry your records, X rays, and such to the hospital or surgery center, an excellent way to avoid delivery snafus during the Y2K inauguration.

Computer problems at your doctor's office, the pharmacy, or your insurer might inhibit access to your records—or even erase them. (The next chapter covers problems with prescription drugs.) Keep a written record of any medications you are taking, with dosages, and any allergies or other key medical information. Carry this with you; it may come in handy when you try to fill a prescription, or in the event of an emergency.

Don't submit paperwork to your insurance company or

Medicare during the Y2K turnover, from roughly mid-December to mid-January. You run a much higher risk of having them swallowed into some giant bureaucratic snarl.

Private physicians are expected to experience few problems with medical equipment. However, billing and appointment systems could be fouled up. You'll want to follow up with your insurer to make sure that your doctor has submitted the necessary paperwork. Take notes of who you spoke with and when.

RESOURCES

■ The Cleveland Clinic Foundation maintains a free collection of literature, both printed and online, that deals with choosing a doctor and a hospital. The Web site is at http://www.ccf.org/pc/quality, or you can call 800-545-7718 to have free guides sent by mail.

SECURE SUFFICIENT PRESCRIPTION DRUGS

BACKGROUND

The supply of medications to the third or so of Americans who use prescription drugs is particularly vulnerable to Y2K glitches. It's a subject the major drug companies don't wish to discuss. They are worried that people will try to stockpile their drugs in anticipation of problems, thus creating a shortage on top of whatever problems computer glitches might create. Few groups that lobby for senior citizens have said much about this either, and there is no federal agency that has taken an interest. Since states regulate the nation's 118,000 pharmacies, the federal government has taken the position that any action should be the responsibility of the states.

WHAT YOU CAN DO

Consider the many ways the flow of prescription drugs could be upset. Shipments of raw materials to drug companies may be curtailed, the factories that make the drugs might have Y2K production problems, transportation could be upset, pharmacies may have trouble with their computers—or those at HMOs, health insurers, or doctors.

Stockpiling your life-sustaining drugs may be the only way to protect yourself. That's not easy to accomplish, however, due to safeguards built into the system. For instance, many drugs are currently restricted by law to a thirty-day supply. And many prescription plans have tough rules about how often a drug can be refilled.

What's more, drugs can be expensive and perishable—making it unwise or financially difficult to build a stockpile. It would make more sense for pharmacies, doctors, and hospitals to build up a Y2K supply. After all, they know what drugs can be substituted for one another and how perishable they are.

But given the health-care industry's lack of interest in the Y2K threat, it doesn't appear that will happen. So talk with your doctor and insurance company about building a small supply of your medication, say two weeks' to thirty days' worth, before the end of 1999.

And be sure to check the dosage and label on any drugs you get from the pharmacy after December 1999. A computer glitch could change the dosage—or even give you the wrong drug. It's critical to know what you are usually taking and to make sure that's what you get from the pharmacy.

Discuss with your doctor what to do if the pharmacy's computer refuses to approve your prescription. That could happen if the computer makes a mistake and thinks you've already got enough supply.

So be sure to ask your doctor to give you copies of your prescriptions as well as phoning them in to the pharmacy or entering them in their computer system.

BONE UP ON EMERGENCY CARE

BACKGROUND

Most people have never had to cope with more than a minor cut or burn on their own. But what if emergency care wasn't readily available? Would you know what to do, or even where to look for advice? Now is the time to assemble a good basic first-aid kit, and to acquire a little knowledge on how to use it. Another must is a basic reference book, which we'll cover in Resources, below. That way, you'll be prepared to cope with the unexpected.

WHAT YOU CAN DO

You'll need to assemble a first-aid kit and keep it in an easily accessible place in your home. A second, smaller kit for your car makes sense too. You can buy a preassembled kit at drugstores and department stores such as Wal-Mart for ten to twenty dollars. Or you can buy the materials to assemble one yourself.

At a minimum, your kit should have adhesive or gauze wrappings in several sizes, bandages in a variety of sizes, surgical tape, soap, sterile gauze, absorbent cotton, tweezers, sharp scissors, cotton-tipped swabs, tissues, thermometer, aspirin or acetaminophen, syrup of ipecac, antiseptic solution and cream, hydrocortisone cream, and elastic wrap.

Here are a few commonsense first-aid rules: Don't move someone who has lost consciousness, or who complains of neck or back pain. Get expert help immediately if the victim complains of sudden chest or abdominal pain, sudden dizziness, severe headache or loss of vision, difficulty breathing or short-ness of breath, severe or persistent vomiting or diarrhea, or sig-nificant bleeding, whether accompanied by pain or not. If bleeding continues for more than a few minutes or after apply-ing pressure to the wound, get help right away. Any wound that becomes inflamed or painful to the touch needs professional attention, as do animal bites of any kind.

Use these most basic first-aid methods:

Bleeding. To stop severe bleeding, lay the victim down with the legs elevated; if possible, elevate the site of the bleed-ing. Remove any debris from the wound and then apply pres-sure directly to the wound using gauze or a clean cloth. Use your hand if there's no cloth available. Maintain pressure until the bleeding stops; if the cloth soaks through, apply another to the top of it. If that fails, you may need to apply a tourniquet, but only as a last resort. This is a strip of cloth or a necktie tied tightly above the wound. Release pressure on the cloth occa-sionally to ensure blood flow to the affected area. Tourniquets must be used if a limb is severed.

Burns. For minor burns, run cool water over the affected areas or submerge it in cool water, though not if you're outside in a cold area. Cover with gauze or bandage. For more serious burns, cover the area with a cool, moist sterile bandage or cloth, but don't use towels or blankets. Don't apply ointments, and get help as soon as possible.

Frostbite. Warm the affected area slowly, but do not rub it. In severe cases, submerge the area in warm but not hot water.

Electrical injury. First, get the person away from the exposed power source, but don't touch a person still in contact with a wire. Use a nonconducting material like a broom or stick to move the wire away from you and the victim. Once that's done, treat any burn. If the person isn't breathing, use CPR.

Carbon monoxide poisoning. Use of space heaters or any fossil-fuel-burning devices, such as an auto, in closed spaces can result in death. The classic warning signs are headache, nausea, or confusion. The skin or lips may be cherry red. The best thing to do is remove the victim from the affected area, and administer oxygen, if available.

Fractures. If you suspect a broken bone, first protect the area from further damage. Immobilize the victim and apply a splint. Pieces of board about the size of the limb are ideal, wrapped with tape or gauze. It that's not available, rolled-up newspapers or magazines may be used. Don't try to straighten the limb; you are simply trying to protect it from further damage.

RESOURCES

No home should be without a comprehensive medical guide that includes first-aid instructions.

■ One of the best is *The Mayo Clinic Family Health Book* (William Morrow and Co., $42.50). This 1,378-page reference volume covers an incredible number of subjects in an easy-to-understand format.

■ Another superior guide is *Johns Hopkins Symptoms and Remedies: The Complete Home Medical Reference* (Random House, $39.95). This comprehensive home medical reference describes a variety of symptoms, ranging from back pain to heart disease, along with helpful guidelines on prevention, the latest therapeutic treatments, and effective medications.

DEMAND ANSWERS ON NATIONAL SECURITY

6

BACKGROUND

The U.S. Department of Defense announced in 1998 that it will indeed be ready for Y2K—but not until 2002. As 1999 approached, the military wasn't even making sure that new systems it *bought* were Y2K compliant. The department's inspector general says this "may seriously hamper the ability of [the defense department] to perform its administrative and war-fighting mission requirements."

It gets scarier. Authorities are investigating whether the nation's strategic defense computers could malfunction because of Y2K computer problems. The government admits that some of its 1.5 million military computers are almost certain to fail after the clock strikes midnight on December 31, 1999.

The military's own inspector general says the Pentagon does not have a complete inventory of its computers, is wasting too much time trying to fix noncritical systems, and has inadequate contingency plans if important systems crash.

Most other governments are even further behind than the United States. Systems in Russia are completely outdated and many must be replaced or taken out of service. EMI Inc., an information-technology consulting firm, says that awareness of the Y2K problem in Russia ranges from none to acknowledging there is a problem but as yet doing nothing to fix it.

What could happen if the armies of the world aren't ready for Y2K? Wars have been started with a single mistake. If defense computers go down, a country may assume it's part of a nuclear attack. The same goes for satellite disruptions. Downed communications networks could also be viewed as a possible attack. Fighter planes could stray into restricted airspace if navigation or air-traffic systems malfunction, triggering retaliation. The list goes on.

WHAT YOU CAN DO

Could the northern hemisphere be incinerated by nuclear weapons launched by some computer mistake, either by the United States, Russia, or some other country? It's extremely unlikely, virtually impossible according to the experts.

Computer experts (who got us into this situation in the first place) say that missiles don't get launched without incredibly complex codes and an ironclad system of checks and double checks. That's true for every nuclear power, including Russia. In fact, computer glitches that Y2K might cause are more likely to freeze machines up, not set them loose firing off missiles. On the other hand, if an enemy wanted to attack the United States, what better time than the stroke of Y2K?

So what can you do? There's only one answer to this question: Demand answers from the politicians in charge, right up to the president. Unless there's a groundswell of public opinion, the Pentagon is likely to continue fixing its computers at a pace that won't get the job done in time.

The United States should consider lending help to other nuclear powers to get their computers ready for Y2K. That would be a wise investment in added security for everyone.

RESOURCES

Send a message to your elected officials.

■ For U.S. House members' mail and e-mail addresses, go to http://www.house.gov/writerep/.

■ Go to http://www.senate.gov/senator/membmail.html for Senate contacts.

■ For information on mailing the president and vice president, go to http://www.whitehouse.gov.

7

STAY SAFE ON NEW YEAR'S EVE

BACKGROUND

The turnover from 1999 to 2000 promises to be the New Year's Eve of a lifetime. After all, you've got to wait another one thousand years for the fourth millennium. But properly speaking, the next millennium doesn't actually begin until 2001, the official start of the twenty-first century. This is because our calendar started with the year 1, not the year 0. So you've got to add one more year to one hundred to reach each new century.

In any case, the Y2K computer bug—or at least worry about Y2K—threatens to spoil the fun. Folks are apt to fall into two camps about this: the partiers who say don't pay a bit of attention to this Y2K stuff, and those cautious people who'd rather not take any chances. (A third group will be oblivious to the whole thing.) Consider your plans for the evening of December 31, 1999, a gauge of your tolerance for risk.

But keep in mind that New Year's celebrations will have an added element of danger. In Los Angeles alone, between 1989 and 1995, thirty-eight people were accidentally killed on New Year's by errant bullets from people firing off guns into the air.

WHAT YOU CAN DO

Early in 1999, travel agents were reporting record bookings for New Year's 2000. Many of those who have made plans to travel probably won't start to worry about Y2K computer problems until media attention focuses on the problems later in 1999. By then it will be too late to get their money back if they decide to stay home.

Some people won't have a choice of plans; they'll be required to report for work December 31. This includes law enforcement, public safety, and emergency personnel. Computer programmers and technicians will be needed at thousands of government and business locations to attend to Y2K glitches. It's a good bet that most hospital and emergency workers will be on-call.

If you're not in these groups, consider staying home and making next year the big celebration—after all, that will be the official start of the new millennium. Neighborhood parties are a great idea, so nobody has to drive, with the worry about traffic signals or power outages, not to mention the drunks who traditionally take to the road despite a Herculean effort to educate the public about the dangers of driving while intoxicated.

The ugly possibilities of riots, power outages, and looting should be enough to introduce a note of caution into your plans. Parents of school-age children planning a night on the town might consider whether a baby-sitter could handle a situation like a power failure or civil unrest.

At this writing, officials planning citywide celebrations that have become so popular hadn't yet announced how they will ensure public safety December 31. Some events may well be canceled; it all depends on the level of public awareness in the days and months leading up to Y2K.

If you plan to be out that evening, give some thought to what you'll do if the worst should happen. How will you get home if the streets are not passable? What will you do if the power fails? How will you contact family members to let them know you're okay if the telephones are not working or the circuits are busy? If you haven't got good answers to these questions, stay close to home.

PROTECT YOUR
HOME AND FAMILY

8 | SURVIVAL BASICS: WATER

BACKGROUND

What if your water or power stops working because of Y2K? What if trucks can't bring food to the stores because the computers that run warehouses and scheduling are down? How will you get by?

It makes sense to do a little planning now, just in case there's trouble. By December 1999 or so, it may be too late. Worried people may well strip the store shelves of basic supplies. And of course that could create a shortage in and of itself, even if Y2K doesn't so much as cause a flicker of trouble.

WHAT YOU CAN DO

The first priority is water. If you have a well that uses a pump, you'll have water only if you have the power to run your electric pump. (Generators are covered in chapter 11.) Water companies are preparing for Y2K but there's still a possibility that the flow will stop.

You may want to store some water just to be on the safe side. This is no small matter when you consider that each person in your family will need about five gallons a day, and that doesn't include bathing. To even store enough water for a week could be an undertaking.

You can fill up your bathtubs on New Year's Eve, and that will give you a fair amount. Plastic milk jugs and pop bottles can be filled (four drops of nonchlorine bleach for two liters will purify the water).

Don't forget your home's hot-water heater will hold up to seventy gallons of water, which you can access by turning the small drain spigot near the bottom of the tank.

If your water supply should become undrinkable, you have several options. Boiling the water for at least ten minutes will eliminate most impurities. Carafe water filters can purify up to a half gallon of water at a time from a pitcher that uses a replaceable filter. Mr. Coffee and Ecowater are two popular brands sold for under $50 and found to be safe and effective by *Consumer Reports*.

Another option is a faucet-mounted filter, also in the $50 range. *Consumer Reports* liked the Culligan Waterware FM-2 and the PUR FM-1000C. The most effective (and most expensive) systems use reverse osmosis; Sears has a system that sells for about $450. Finally, camping equipment stores stock small handheld devices for $100 or less that can filter common pollutants from a limited quantity of water.

RESOURCES
See chapter 10.

9 | SURVIVAL BASICS: FOOD

BACKGROUND

Our food supply network is just in time these days; grocery stores at most keep food on the shelves only seventy-two hours. They restock as needed with daily deliveries, mostly by truck. When the public figures out that it might be a good idea to prepare, there could be a last-minute rush, so start stocking up several months early.

WHAT YOU CAN DO

You could run down to the supermarket and get lots of prepared foods like soups and packaged goods, but it makes more sense to stock basic ingredients so you can make your own meals fresh. And if Y2K turns out to be completely smooth, you can use this stuff rather than ignoring it on your shelves until the next millennium.

Your shopping list should include staples such as flour, sugar, cooking oil, powdered eggs and milk, dried pasta, rice, and dried cereals. Canned tuna, salmon, and shrimp will come in handy. Go easy on dried meats, which can be expensive, not very nutritious, and quite salty.

Buy extra food a little at a time in the months leading up to 2000. Eat your older supplies first so stuff in the back doesn't get stale. Consider purchasing a food dehydrator. You can get one for $100 or so that can dry up and package lots of fresh foods for ultralong storage. This will come in handy, Y2K shortage or not. Dried fruits are especially nice to have come winter.

Storing food safely means: Keeping the food cool; the storage lives of most foods are cut in half by every increase of 18° F. Low humidity is important, too. Keep the storage area air-conditioned and dehumidified during the humid times of the year. Use packaging that protects against moisture. All containers should be kept off the floor and out of direct contact from exterior walls to reduce condensation. Food should be kept out of the light, especially sunlight. Be sure to use the First In, First Out (FIFO) method for rotating your storage.

RESOURCES
See chapter 10.

10 | SURVIVAL BASICS: SHELTER

BACKGROUND

Shelter in January is a big concern in most of the United States. If the power goes out, your furnace won't work even if it burns oil or gas.

That's because electric pumps are used for the blower or to circulate the hot water. Extra blankets will get you through the night, but the utmost caution is needed to avoid injury from alternative heat sources.

WHAT YOU CAN DO

First, a few words of caution. Don't turn on the gas stove burners to get heat. They release deadly carbon monoxide and the open flame robs oxygen from your breathing air. Ditto for kerosene heaters; hundreds of people have died from inhaling the exhaust from these unvented devices.

If your home has a fireplace, it can be altered to give off a significant amount of heat. That could help you if the power goes out, and you could also use the fireplace to cut your winter heating bills. A fireplace heat exchanger can cost as little as a few hundred dollars. Such a device takes the hot air from your fireplace and blows it into your home. A conventional fireplace is a poor heating device; more than 80 percent of the heat from the fire goes up the chimney. A woodstove or heating supply dealer can sell you a fireplace heat exchanger.

Coal- and wood-burning stoves are another popular heating

alternative. These can be installed in an existing fireplace, or as a stand-alone unit. A good stove can easily heat one thousand square feet of space. The cost of a basic unit, with installation, can be under $1,000.

A propane or natural gas fireplace or stove has the added charm of an attractive logset with flame. Many newer models are specially designed to be installed without a stack or vent, in homes with sufficient airflow. The installed price is $750 to $1,500 or more, but most models don't need electricity to operate.

Most gas- and oil-fired furnaces won't operate if electric service is disrupted. However, a professional electrician can wire a furnace (or your home's main electric service panel) to safely accept power from a portable generator. That way, you can heat your home "off the grid" should the need arise.

RESOURCES
Books
■ *Back to Basics: How to Learn and Enjoy Traditional American Skills* (Reader's Digest, $26.95) was first published in 1981 and recently updated. It's all about a simpler life and making things by hand.

■ *The Encyclopedia of Country Living: An Old Fashioned Recipe Book* by Carla Emery (Country Living Books, $27.95) is an old standard of recipes, instructions, and practical advice on all aspects of growing and preparing food.

Web Sites
■ Many Web sites on survival and simple living can by found at http://members.aol.com/rafleet/survivalring.htm. This Web ring consists primarily of personal home pages of varying quality.

■ An extensive group of Web pages related to self-sufficiency in food, energy, and home can be found at www.coolpages.net/2000/survival.

CONSIDER AN ELECTRIC GENERATOR

11

BACKGROUND

Companies that make portable electric generators expect 1999 to be their best year ever as consumers snap up these products in anticipation of Y2K power outages. At the end of 1998, experts were predicting that 25 percent of the nation's power grid will go down after December 31, 1999. That, in turn, could cause still more outages as the remaining links in the system must bear increased demand.

Generators come in a wide variety of sizes and vary in cost from about $300 all the way up to $2,000 or more. Generators use gasoline or propane to produce electricity, and all of them are meant for use outdoors. They're generally noisy and incapable of powering many appliances, but if the power goes out come Y2K—or at any time, for that matter—you'll thank your lucky stars you've got one. Generators are handy for running electric devices at work sites, or in the yard.

WHAT YOU CAN DO

First figure out how big a generator you need. A lightbulb requires 100 watts of power, a television 200. But appliances with compressors, like refrigerators, need much more. Though a refrigerator may operate on 1,000 watts, it may need 1,800 "surge power" watts just for when the compressor kicks in. A 3,000- to 5,000-watt generator will fill your basic needs; it won't run your whole house, but it will supply the minimum power necessary. That could include a refrigerator, a handful of lightbulbs, and perhaps a few other low-current appliances. Such devices as hot-water heaters, electric stoves, and clothes dryers draw too much high-voltage current to be operated by conventional generators.

Gasoline powers the large majority of the small engines in generators, though diesel and liquid propane generators are available. The more watts the generator produces, the more fuel you need. Most generators burn a little less than a gallon an hour. For a week, that's around forty gallons of fuel for a good-size generator. Figure you can store some gas in containers and siphon the rest you'll need from your vehicles. Be sure to store gas in approved containers in well-ventilated areas.

Gas gets stale with extended storage, so replace it every six months to a year by pouring it into your vehicle tanks and refilling the cans with fresh fuel. Gasoline stabilizer additives are available for longer-term storage.

Generators are available from hardware stores, Sears, Home Depot, Sams, BJ's, mail order, and RV stores. But don't wait until 2000 is almost here before you shop, you could be disappointed.

You'll need heavy gauge (#10 and above), well-made extension cords to bring the electricity to your appliances. Do not run the wires through puddles or under carpets or rugs. If you want to hook a generator to your house current, call a qualified electrician. Do not attempt an installation or you could hurt yourself or a utility worker, or destroy your house.

KEEP TRACK OF YOUR MAIL

12

BACKGROUND

We take it for granted the mail will arrive when it's supposed to, or at least in the same week or so that it's supposed to. Wind, rain, sleet, and snow may not stop the letter carriers from their appointed rounds, but the Y2K bug threatens to do just that.

The U.S. Postal Service is extremely concerned about the extra stress the approach of the new millennium will put on its already overtaxed resources. Since the Y2K bug could put at risk electronic transfers of data and money in some parts of the nation and abroad, businesses and government groups are looking to the postal service as a backup delivery system if their computers malfunction.

The postmaster general calls this "an increasing concern" that could "seriously challenge postal operations." Officials are worried they may be swamped with letters and packages lacking bar codes if the computer systems used by bulk mailers collapse. The codes are critical to speeding parcels through mail processing plants.

The post office has its plate of Y2K problems, and it's full. Mail processing depends on about fifty computer systems operating in 250 plants across the country. More than 100,000 personal computers, mainframes, and other hardware and software must be analyzed for Y2K problems. Whether this can all be done in time is anybody's guess. But even a fully functioning postal service can't handle much additional capacity during December, traditionally its busiest month.

What You Can Do

Unfortunately, the buildup to Y2K will happen just at the time of maximum strain on public and private delivery services. It's wise to assume that the extra volume of packages and letters will cause massive delays in delivery.

So plan accordingly. Get those holiday cards out no later than the end of November. Post your December bills at the beginning of the month, not the end.

If you normally send holiday gifts by mail, allow an extra three to six weeks for delivery. That means you should mail them out just after Thanksgiving. If you send packages overseas by surface mail, ship them off no later than the beginning of September.

Private delivery services may be the only alternative if you want to be sure of prompt delivery (see Resources, below). During the 1997 United Parcel Service strike, the major delivery companies wisely declined to accept more packages than they could handle, so it's a good bet they will refuse to take your package if it can't be delivered on time.

If you rely on the mail for vital supplies, such as prescription medicine or items crucial to your business, make other arrangements for December and January.

E-mail is another alternative for holiday cards and messages this year. You can design your own cards on free Internet sites and send them as e-mail. Services such as America Online make this easier by supplying software that will open these attachments.

Resources

■ The major private delivery services are: Federal Express (800-463-3339), Airborne Express (800-247-2676), Emery Worldwide (800-443-6379), and United Parcel Service (800-742-5877).

■ You don't need your own computer or an Internet service provider to send and receive e-mail. Just sign on to the Internet at your local library and log on to http://www.hotmail.com. There you will find instructions on setting up a free account to send and receive e-mail.

■ You can design and send free electronic greeting cards and messages by signing on to Hallmark Connections at http://www.hallmark.com. Many of the cards are free.

■ Blue Mountain Arts, at http://www.bluemountain.com, features Java-animated electronic card designs for Christmas, Hanukkah, Kwanzaa, and even Ramadan.

■ Kodak, at http://www.kodak.com/digitalimaging/, lets you transfer a photo onto a Kodak greeting card.

13 PLAN ALTERNATIVES TO THE TELEPHONE

BACKGROUND

The complex networks that we rely on for voice and data transmissions contain thousands of computers, switches, and other devices with microchips. Some of these are certain to fail come January 1, 2000.

The U.S. telecommunications industry is actually a complex network of over 1,100 small independent telephone companies and nearly 5,000 mostly small Internet service providers. These companies rely on one anothers' circuits and switching equipment to complete voice and data calls. If even a small percentage of these companies aren't ready for Y2K, service could be disrupted. That doesn't even take into account overseas telephone networks, whose Y2K readiness ranges from pretty good to abysmal.

Don't assume that just because you get service from one of the big carriers such as AT&T, Bell Atlantic, or GTE, you'll be okay. The interconnected nature of the telecommunications network makes it almost impossible to determine if your telephone service will be interrupted after Y2K. Even if your local and long-distance carriers are totally prepared, some other link in the chain—either here or overseas—may bring them down.

Cellular service could also be affected, though there's no telling if the cell networks themselves will be affected or the landlines that they connect to.

The bottom line is that you may pick up your phone and find no dial tone, no long-distance service, or busy circuits. The implications are enormous: Think about how much we depend on 911, for example. No phone service also means no e-mail, Internet, or any other online services.

What You Can Do

In case your phone service is disrupted, make plans long before January 1 to back up vital communications. If your phone doesn't work, put your emergency plan into action. Designate someone to check up on the elderly or infirm; make fall-back plans to convey important messages by other means.

Forget about using Western Union for messages. The days of messenger service are gone; they use the post office to deliver telegrams, and it's quite possible that postal operations will also be disrupted.

Remember citizens band radios? Some think CBs will stage a comeback. CBs can operate by battery, with a range of several miles, even farther with a rooftop antenna. Plus, there's no monthly charges because they use the public airwaves.

Start placing your keep-in-touch calls to far-flung friends and relations several weeks before the new year. Call volume in the second half of December is expected to break records worldwide, so you may get the "all circuits busy" signal if you wait too long to call.

Find out where your emergency services are located. Where's the nearest hospital or emergency-care center? The nearest police and ambulance? You'll have to drive there in an emergency if the telephone service is disrupted.

14 GET YOUR HOME APPLIANCES Y2K READY

Background

Many home appliances manufactured in the 1990s contain microchips. Some of these chips have a date function that's not going to work after December 31, 1999. This includes VCRs, coffeemakers, microwave and conventional ovens, camcorders, thermostats, sprinkler systems—the list goes on. Some appliances that have no obvious date function may still have date-related circuitry built into them.

When the Federal Trade Commission asked manufacturers about Y2K, here is what the Consumer Electronics Manufacturers Association said: "Essentially all consumer electronics products currently being sold, and a vast majority of consumer electronics products sold in the past, will not experience Y2K problems."

A "limited number of older models" will not be able to handle the '00 date, such as camcorders and VCRs. But these machines should work just fine otherwise. Vacuums, dishwashers, and a few other appliances may have a Y2K date problem. Some medical devices used at home may require special attention.

What You Can Do

At worst, Y2K will cause minor inconveniences around the home, most of which you can safely ignore, such as the date on your coffeemaker display. Older VCRs that can't recognize 2000 probably won't be able to record programs in advance. You can trick such machines into performing this function by using another year in the date calendar (1972 uses the same calendar as 2000). In any case, VCRs are almost a commodity item these days; you can get a basic one for under $150. A cheaper alternative is to buy a VCR Plus device, which records programs independently of the VCR, turning the machine on and off as needed by use of a six-digit code for each program.

Your home videos may be forever stuck in the 1990s, but you can turn off the date function on most video-camera models. Satellite TV programming providers say they will automatically download software commands to address the new date. With other appliances, it's best to wait and see if there's a problem.

One exception: fancy electronic setback thermostats. You don't want the heat to stop working in January. If your thermostat has a full date setting, try entering a date in '00 to see what happens. If this does not compute, you can simply set the date back a year or two, or contact the manufacturer about a fix.

Certain home medical devices may need attention, such as cardiac monitors, IV drip machines, and drug delivery devices. By all means contact your doctor if you own any such device.

Older fax machines probably won't accept the '00 date, but they can still be used by turning the date back. However, keep in mind that any documents you fax or receive will be imprinted with the wrong date.

Could your vacuum cleaner or some other appliance cease functioning? That's possible but highly unlikely. If there is a problem, there's nothing you can do because such devices contain embedded microchips, the type that can't be reprogrammed. However, it's likely that the manufacturer of any such appliance will correct the problem—or face lots of irate customers as well as the threat of class-action lawsuits.

Wristwatches with full calendar functions may not be able to handle the new date. If the watch cost more than $100, take it to a jeweler to see if it can be updated.

If your device can accept the date 1972, you're in luck. The years 2000 and 1972 use the same calendar, so the correct date and day of the week will be displayed. For 2001, you can use 1990.

RESOURCES

■ Information about electronic appliances is available from the Consumer Electronics Manufacturers Association at http://www.cema.com.

■ *Consumer Reports* magazine maintains a large database of manufacturers' telephone numbers. You can check back issues at your local library or get the information online at http://www.consumerreports.org.

■ All the major appliance makers have Web sites, and many of them have included Y2K information. Try typing the name of the manufacturer into your Web browser or using a search engine like Yahoo! or Excite.

ATTENTION: APARTMENT, CO-OP, AND CONDO DWELLERS

15

BACKGROUND

If you live in an apartment-style dwelling or part of a planned community, don't assume somebody's going to take care of you if Y2K shuts down power or other vital systems. Landlords of small buildings may not have the slightest clue there could even be a problem. Co-op and condo boards, usually run by volunteers, can't be expected to have much Y2K savvy either. That leaves you, the person who's most directly affected, to make sure your comfort and security are maintained.

WHAT YOU CAN DO

Those responsible for multiunit buildings, apartment houses, co-ops, and condominiums must take basic action now to avoid the need for hasty—and expensive—remedial action later. Every building has to have a plan, which should begin with a comprehensive audit of all date-sensitive functions. That plan must make assumptions about what could happen if services are disrupted. For larger buildings, vendors will likely have to be hired to conduct this investigation and fix any problems.

Elevators are a big concern; some may stop functioning at midnight December 31 due to either a computer or power failure. Experts say that elevators have safety devices that will stop them from falling in such an emergency, but people can get stuck inside. Potential problems could occur with security systems, fire alarms, smoke alarms, thermostats, and even heating, ventilation, and air-conditioning equipment.

In many large buildings even backup electrical generators are controlled by computers. To find out if there will be problems, managing boards need to contact the vendor who sold or services the system to determine whether it's Y2K compliant. That may be nearly impossible at the last minute, which in the case of Y2K could be anytime after November 1999.

Other systems to examine include buildingwide intercom or telephone systems, keycard entry systems, garage doors, sprinklers, and lighting systems. Even thermostats in individual apartments may have chips in them that could stop working.

Vendors should be contacted, such as heating-oil companies, which use computer programs to schedule deliveries. Just about every vendor the managing board uses during the year should be reviewed for possible Y2K compliance problems.

Apartment dwellers should take stock of their living quarters, their floor, and the fire escapes. Make sure you know the exit in case of emergency, without using the elevator. Measure off the paces from your apartment to the fire exit and write them down just in case the power and emergency lighting fail. Try the fire escape route to count the number of floors and look for any obstructions. Check out any systems in your apartment that may contain computer chips, such as heating/cooling, communications, alarms, and detectors.

Finally, when December 31 arrives, stay out of elevators and public areas. Have a flashlight, preferably a stand-up lantern-style one, and candles ready in case the power goes out. Get some spare batteries as well. Make plans with neighbors to check on one another.

But most important, get after your board or managing agent to make sure they've made the building Y2K compliant.

GET TO KNOW YOUR NEIGHBORS

16

BACKGROUND

The old saw that good fences make good neighbors is the sort of thinking that keeps people confined to their own little world. It's a well-known fact that communities with good neighbors make better places to live. If there's civil upset come Y2K, you'll need to band together, and that's where neighbors will come in handy. But good neighbors will make your life better all year round.

WHAT YOU CAN DO

Go on over next door and introduce yourself. Let your neighbors know that you'll be watching out for them. In turn, they'll want to watch out for you.

Bring the conversation around to Y2K and ask what they think. You'll probably find out most of your neighbors are as concerned as you are.

In cities and towns where there are neighborhood block watch groups, Y2K is an obvious subject for discussion. These are groups whose goal is to keep their eyes open and report any suspicious activity to the police. Areas with block watch signs posted do have lower crime rates. Contact your local police department for help in setting up a block watch.

Groups of neighbors can share information about Y2K preparedness. In the event of utility outages or civil unrest, neighbors can band together to patrol and watch out for one another, report suspicious activity to the police, and even pool resources.

Responsibility for preparedness materials can be divided among neighbors, easing the burden on everyone. Best of all, any planning you do can be tailored to other emergency situations, such as floods, tornadoes, and so forth.

Of course, the best advice for getting good neighbors is to be one yourself. Good neighbors are those folks who pick up litter on the street, even though it is not in front of their own house. They will shovel your walk when you are sick or watch your kids in a pinch. They take care of the little things that make a big difference in daily life.

BACKGROUND

With the possibility that Y2K computer foul-ups could erase or make unavailable your important records, it's a good idea to obtain copies now and store them in a safe place. You'll be glad you did next time you need a document. Make sure to get copies of documents for your children, elderly parents, or other dependents.

WHAT YOU CAN DO

Secure copies of the following documents:

Birth certificate

Social Security card

Marriage license/certificate

Religious records (baptism, confirmation, etc.)

Deeds, titles, insurance policies, pensions

Mortgage, credit card, and all other loan agreements

Tax returns, W-2s, 1099s, IRS agreements, etc.

Educational records, diplomas, etc.

You've probably already got most of these scattered about your house. If you need copies, write to the correct jurisdiction and request a certified copy. There will probably be a small fee. Store these documents in a safe place on your property or in a private depository. An inexpensive fireproof lock box is an excellent repository.

If you haven't done so already, make a duplicate of your computer files. You can do this by purchasing a Zip drive, which sells for less than $200. Or at least use floppy disks to make copies of your most important documents, well before Y2K.

Voice mail could be wiped out, so be sure to listen to any stored messages by December 30. Read any unopened e-mails by that time as well.

EXPLAIN Y2K TO YOUR FAMILY

18

BACKGROUND

It's easy to be intimidated by Year 2000 talk, with its emphasis on protection and techno-computer lingo. Chances are one person in your household is more computer literate than the rest. It's important for that person to bring everyone else in the family up to speed—especially the children—regarding whatever challenges the Y2K computer problem may bring.

WHAT YOU CAN DO

Obviously anyone can act on the information in these pages. If you are the computer-aware person in the family, don't get all wrapped up in the how-to aspects of Y2K preparation. It's up to you to help put things in perspective.

The first thing you can do is talk to your children about the problem. They'll want to know what blackouts and shortages are all about. Assure them there's nothing to be worried about or afraid of, and that you're taking precautions just in case. Tell them your preparations are going to make them safer, in the same way you've cautioned them about crossing the street safely, not playing with fire, and so forth. (It's a good idea to involve children in some Y2K preparations.)

Show your children how to escape from the house if there's an emergency. Depending on their ages, kids already know enough about bad things that can happen, but you might want to go over the possibilities, such as fires, power outages, intruders, and the like.

What if one of the adults in the household thinks anything to do with Y2K is a waste of time? Or what if one partner is obsessed with preparing? Many couples may disagree on the extent of the problem and what preparations are really necessary. Perhaps one partner wants to turn the house into an armed encampment, complete with a basement shelter. The other thinks that's overreacting. Like any other important issue couples face, you'll have to talk it over and find some middle ground.

It's probably better to err on the side of caution in any case. One way to ensure domestic harmony is to find an unobtrusive place for any items you acquire, like extra food or a generator. Most people hate the idea of extra stuff cluttering up the living space.

Perhaps a member of the family is keen on keeping guns in the house for protection. If that's a fait accompli, the best you can do is make double sure all the precautions are observed, and that your children are instructed to stay away from weapons—and they know what to do if they find one. Make sure the gun has a trigger lock and the gun itself is in a locked place—with the ammunition stored elsewhere, also under lock and key.

What if your spouse thinks you're crazy to be concerned about Y2K? It's up to you to explain the situation and back up what you're saying with whatever resources you can muster. But if in the final analysis your partner won't have anything to do with it, go ahead and make whatever preparations you want. Just ask your spouse to humor you; it's all for your peace of mind.

RESOURCES

■ The Web site Y2K Women, at http://www.y2kwomen.com, run by Karen Anderson, a family counselor, is geared toward women. There's a question-and-answer section, bulletin boards, and a chat room. Here you can find tips on how to talk to your family and to other women about Y2K.

BECOME MORE SELF-SUFFICIENT

BACKGROUND

The Y2K bug and the possibility of disruption in utility services has sparked new interest in "sustainable living" products, items that allow people to survive for weeks or even months "off the grid." Stores that sell such items are reporting record sales. We're not suggesting that you need to run out and buy a lot of expensive gadgets to survive Y2K. You might, however, consider earth-friendly goods as a matter of course when you buy.

You'll save money in operating costs, use less of the earth's resources, and you'll be ready if Y2K or some other disaster, natural or man-made, knocks out your technological lifelines.

WHAT YOU CAN DO

If enough homes switched to low-energy-consumption products, there would be no power shortage come Y2K even if a quarter of the electrical grid capacity is downed.

The first thing you can do is change over your lighting from "standard" incandescents to compact fluorescents (CF) and halogen bulbs. You can get 75 watts' worth of light with 20 watts of electricity with a CF. This one move can reduce your electrical usage by 10 to 20 percent. Just one bulb during the course of its long life will save $40 to $50. That same bulb will save 630 pounds of coal or 51 gallons of oil from being burned. The other key thing you can do is replace old appliances. A typical older refrigerator can use 100 kwh of electricity per month, compared to as few as 20 kwh for new models. Switching from an electric hot-water heater to a gas tankless one could save as much as $30 per month. Other ideas include:

Solar panels. If you live in a sunny part of the country, have a look at solar panels. At about $400 each, these panels can supply much of the power needs of a typical household. They can be installed on the roof and need no maintenance. Systems can be designed for homes that get as little as five hours per day of sunlight, though payback will take much longer in northern areas.

Wind generators. These are available for less than $750 and can supply 400 or more peak watts of power under high wind conditions and arctic cold. At that rate, you could pay back the cost in as few as five years.

With either system, you charge a bank of batteries, which supplies electricity to an inverter. The inverter will interface with the utility company, which is required by law to buy any excess power from you.

Sewage. You can get a composting toilet for less than $1,000 that has no odor and gives you free fertilizer.

Household appliances. You can cook with a reflector-powered Solar Chef "sun oven" for $385. A power-saving Creda EcoWash ($900) and EcoDry ($692) use a fraction of the power and water that conventional machines do. The crank-powered short-wave "FreePlay" radio from Baygen at $100 has excellent sound and generates its own power with an occasional turn of the crank.

RESOURCES

■ The company Jade Mountain sells a full line of the type of products discussed here. They maintain an Internet site at http://www.jademountain.com.

■ A Web site with links to all kinds of alternative energy and sustainable living sites can be found at http://www.webconx.com/survive2k/.

20 | RURAL FOLKS GET READY

BACKGROUND

So you live away from the big cities with their wall-to-wall computers. Don't think for a moment your life won't be affected by Y2K. Anybody involved in agriculture has plenty to worry about, and so do those who live in rural areas. First of all, utility companies in less-populated areas are the furthest behind in solving their computer problems, so residents of sparsely populated areas have the highest chance of losing power and/or telephone service come the chilly winds of January 1, 2000.

On farms, some types of farm equipment, including high-tech planting and feeding machines, may encounter Y2K glitches. Pumps with computerized date timers may cease to work. If the power goes out, milking machines won't operate. The paperwork end of farming could be thrust into even greater disarray: U.S. Department of Agriculture computers may not be able to process commodity pricing or loan information; payments to grain producers might be delayed. And there's worry that the many outside vendors that farms deal with won't be ready, causing inconvenience and delay.

WHAT YOU CAN DO

Residents of isolated areas, much more so than their urban counterparts, would do well to make plans to be self-sufficient for a spell. Lay in supplies of canned and packaged goods, and plenty of water (covered in chapters 8 and 9). A simple power generator may be worth the $500 to $750 investment, covered in chapter 11. Electric heaters are woefully inadequate in the chilly north, assuming you've got the power to operate one. And make sure any fossil-fuel heating devices are adequately ventilated.

Farms are far too complex to address with any detail here. But farmers should contact the companies that have manufactured their key electronic equipment to ask if the devices are Y2K compliant. If you can't get these machines fixed in time, make plans for backups. Contact your Farm Bureau for advice on billing, payments, and the like.

Long before January 1, your local government should have held meetings to discuss Y2K preparedness. If they haven't by the time you read this, it's time to get on the phone (while it still works) and get things rolling.

KEEP YOUR COMPUTER
FROM CRASHING

MAKE YOUR PC COMPLIANT, STEP 1

BACKGROUND

Corporate computer systems may have millions of lines of code to fix, but making most home computers Y2K compliant isn't hard at all. You don't need to spend a fortune for technicians to do the job either. Just follow the directions here, and by using a few simple tools, from the Internet for free or by purchasing inexpensive software, you'll be able to solve most problems yourself. Macintosh users don't need to do much; Mac clocks are good until at least 2040, though this isn't to say that some software applications won't give you problems.

WHAT YOU CAN DO

Here's the first of three steps to diagnosing and fixing a PC Year 2000 problem. The hardware—that's the microchips and other devices that make up the piping and brain of your computer—is centered on the BIOS, or the basic input/output system. The BIOS tells your computer what to do, and if it won't handle the 2000 date, the computer may not operate correctly because it passes on the date to the software, like spreadsheet and word processing programs.

The operating system software, such as Windows, may fix a BIOS problem on its own. One sure way to tell is to call the manufacturer of your computer and ask. PCs in service before 1998 have a higher likelihood of problems. You can also test the BIOS for Y2K compliance using special software (see Resources in chapter 23). Another way to test your computer is by entering the '00 date in the time and date control panel and then restarting the machine to see what happens. If the computer won't boot up with the new date, reboot and type in a date earlier than 2000 and you'll be back where you started.

If you run the test using the special software, you'll get one of three diagnoses. The first is all okay (though that doesn't include software, which we'll cover later) or, two, you need a BIOS upgrade. Don't panic if you need an upgrade. The Resources section in chapter 23 shows you where to get this for free or at little cost. It just takes a minute to install the upgrade; very few computers are not upgradable. The third—and most likely—message you may get is that your computer's BIOS needs a little attention when you first start it up in 2000.

On that day, all you have to do is start up the machine but don't open any applications or documents. On older machines, display your DOS prompt and type "date." Simply type in the new current date. You can do this in Windows by selecting Start/Run then typing "command."

Okay, but you're not out of the woods yet. See the next chapter for advice on diagnosing and fixing Y2K problems with your computer's operating system.

If you do take your computer in for Y2K repairs, get a written estimate before any work is done. Use a factory-authorized repair shop and don't spend more than the machine is worth. (That may not be much, since used computers are usually worth about 10 percent of their retail price.)

BACKGROUND

In step 1, we showed you how to figure out whether your computer's brain, called the BIOS chip, needs a Y2K update and how to accomplish that. Once you have that problem licked, you have to determine whether the operating system, such as Windows 95 or Windows 98, has a Y2K problem. If it does, this is usually a simple fix that will only require a few minutes of your time. Microsoft makes operating systems for 99 percent of the personal computers in use by consumers today, and unfortunately, even the latest version, Windows 98, needs a little bit of help to be Y2K compliant. Older systems such as Windows 3.1 need more attention than we can go into here, so consult Resources, below, for help.

WHAT YOU CAN DO

In Windows 95, the Windows Explorer will recognize Year 2000 only if you go to the Control Panel and change the Regional Settings by typing in the date. This can be done after January 1, 2000. If you are using Windows File Manager, included with some Windows 95 operating systems, it gets more complicated. You'll need a software update, which can be obtained from Microsoft (see Resources, below.)

According to Microsoft, Windows 98 is fully Y2K compliant. Well, almost. You'll still need to set the Control Panel's Regional Settings to handle four-digit entries for the new year. If you're using Windows NT Workstation, which is mostly for commercial users, you'll need to download a series of patches called NT Service Pack 3 that will bring this operating system into full compliance.

You're almost done now. Go to step 3, the next chapter, for advice on what to do about software, those application programs such as Microsoft Excel and Word, to make sure they are Y2K compatible.

RESOURCES

■ Everything you need to fix Windows 95 and 98 is available on the Internet at http://www.microsoft.com, and almost all of it is free. Click on Microsoft's Year 2000 resource center. If you aren't on the Net, you can call Microsoft at 800-425-9400 to ask questions and order products.

■ For older operating systems, try Microsoft first, but you may have more luck at Web sites of companies that specialize in this area. You can find links to these vendors at http://www.pcmag. com/y2k, run by *PC Magazine*. Or try www.zdnet.com/y2k, which has links to lots of resource sites. That site is sponsored by Ziff-Davis, a major publisher of computer magazines. If you're not on the Internet, see your computer dealer.

23 MAKE YOUR PC SOFTWARE Y2K COMPATIBLE, STEP 3

BACKGROUND

In steps 1 and 2 we showed you how to diagnose and fix your computer's BIOS and operating system. The final, and most complicated, step is figuring out whether your computer's software needs attention. Why is this important? Many kinds of software interact with your computer's operating system and outside sources of information, other programs, or the Internet. Any weak link in the chain can cause your computer to generate errors or stop working.

All the big software companies have developed patches—little bits of code you can put on your computer—to solve the Y2K problem. For most people, obtaining these patches for their application programs will suffice. But heavy-duty computer users who have attached plug-ins and shareware files (free software from the Internet) may have additional problems.

WHAT YOU CAN DO

You can test your machine by entering January 1, 2000, in the date field, but we don't recommend this unless you back up all the files on your hard drive first. The casual computer user won't be able to accomplish this, so it's best to wait until after January 1 to see if any of the applications have a problem. With most word processing software, games, and the like, there should be no problem.

But spreadsheets and databases, which have calendar functions built in, may cause your computer to malfunction. You can contact the manufacturer of the software for help. Microsoft's Web site has many software fixes for its products, as do all the other big software makers. (For phone numbers and Web sites, see Resources, below.)

Your other option is to purchase and install a program that will test your software; some of these test your operating system and BIOS as well.

A last resort—or a first one for the technically disinclined— is to purchase the latest version of your favorite software programs. You'll save some money by purchasing upgrades rather than a new full software package.

RESOURCES
Software Makers
■ **Corel.** Makes Paradox and Quattro Pro; www.corel.com. 800-772-6735.

■ **Lotus.** Makes Lotus 1-2-3 and Approach; www.lotus.com. 800-343-5414.

■ **Microsoft.** Many applications, including Outlook, Access, Excel, and Money; www.microsoft.com/2000; 800-426-9400.

■ **Intuit.** Makes Quicken for Windows and Macintosh; www.intuit.com. 800-446-8848.

Testing Programs
■ McAfee 2000 Toolbox ($29.95; 800-332-9966) checks software and BIOS, and offers some ways to get around or fix both, and links to Web sites and resources that can provide a fix.

■ Check 2000 PC ($49; 703-908-6600) is a comprehensive tool to diagnose and fix all Y2K aspects of your computer.

BACKGROUND

The Internet is a wild and woolly frontier where something like three million new pages are being added every day. It stretches all over the planet and is used by 150 million or more people a day. Experts think the coming of Y2K needn't be a trauma to the Internet, though there will probably be isolated outages and malfunctions.

Your gateway to the Internet, which could be an Internet service provider (ISP) or an online service such as America Online, may encounter Y2K glitches. So could the telephone company that provides the lines that connect you. Or one of the many servers worldwide that tie the Internet together may malfunction. Individual Internet sites themselves could go down for any number of reasons. Power outages could cause any of these to go down. In other words, don't bank on business as usual on the Internet come January 1, 2000.

WHAT YOU CAN DO

Both Netscape and Microsoft, makers of the two major Internet browsers, the application programs that you use to surf the Net, are designing new versions of their software that will be Y2K compliant. It makes sense to upgrade your browser before January 1, 2000—or before you start surfing the Web in 2000. You can do this for free; see Resources, below.

As for going online January 1 and beyond, surf at your own risk. Be especially careful about downloading application programs from the Internet that may not be Y2K compliant. Unless there's some assurance that the software is compliant, don't download it. You risk crashing your computer.

It's a good idea to call any vendor you deal with to verify that transactions you make over the Internet, such as purchases, online banking, and brokerage accounts, have actually been received. Decline to do business with Internet merchants that fail to post a telephone number to handle customer inquiries.

Ask your bank and broker about Y2K-compliant versions of their software as well.

Don't worry about your computer being infected by some Y2K virus if you use the Internet after January 1. The only possibility this can happen is if you download application files from the Internet.

Security of private information such as credit card numbers is a special concern. Y2K glitches could conceivably let hackers into previously secure networks. To avoid trouble, don't use the Internet for commerce until it's clear that such problems won't be a concern.

RESOURCES

■ The latest version of the Netscape Navigator browser is available at http://www.netscape.com. It's free, though downloading could take an hour or more over a slow modem connection (less than 28.8KPS).

■ Microsoft's Internet Explorer browser can be downloaded free from http://www.microsoft.com/explorer.

Both browsers can be purchased at many computer software stores.

25

BEWARE THESE TROUBLESOME DATES

BACKGROUND

January 1, 2000, isn't the only date that can cause problems for computers and other devices. While the Y2K problem has been largely perceived as a single event that will occur January 1, 2000, it has become clear that the bug is part of a series of crashes that will strike for months before, and maybe years after, that date.

The second biggest date problem will occur at the end of February 2000. That's because the Year 2000 is an out-of-sequence leap year. Here's why: Every four years is a leap year, meaning an extra day is added to February to make up for the slight difference between the 365.24 days of the solar year and the usual 365 days of the Gregorian calendar. Thus, if a year is evenly divisible by four, it is a leap year—this extra day nearly brings the two time systems in line. However, to make up for the remaining difference, a second rule requires the calendar to skip a leap year every one hundred years, by convention at the turn of each century. But a third rule also applies: Every four centuries, a non–leap year becomes a leap year. This rule applies to the Year 2000, making it a leap year.

WHAT YOU CAN DO

On September 9, 1999, and perhaps long after that date, be on the lookout for errors in billings and other material you receive from businesses. The reason for the error is that 9/9/99, besides being the date, is also a computer "red flag" for the old-style use of strings of 9s as special program markers. That may cause problems with some computers as software may not be able to tell whether the numbers are a date or a marker.

Just two months after January 1, some programs will begin to sputter again, this time over whether or not 2000 is a leap year. It is a leap year, although as we discussed above, the reasons for this are complicated. Practically any device you own that has a calendar function will have to be reset to recognize this extra day, including most personal computers. (When you start up your machine after February 28, if the date is incorrect, simply open the appropriate window and enter the correct date.)

You'll want to check your savings accounts and CDs to make sure that you've been credited an extra day of interest for February. Be sure to reconfirm any reservations or appointments you have for that date and after; there's a chance that computerized systems will be a day behind in their record-keeping.

Other dates with destiny:

August 22, 1999: the end of the first 1,024-week cycle for the Global Positioning System network. (Covered in chapter 42.)

April 1, 2001: A bug in the Windows family of operating systems will appear. Thought to affect programs running under Windows 95, 98, and NT, the bug causes the software to think it is one hour earlier than the correct time displayed on the Windows clock. It will cause the glitch to continue for one week, until April 8, 2001. The bug is likely to cause significant problems for programs that work on very precise timing data, such as hotel wake-up call systems.

January 19, 2038: the end of the 32-bit Unix time cycle. The operating system for thousands of corporate computers will not accept any dates past this point.

January 1, 10000: Y10K failure. Programs that use four-digit years will fail. (You don't need to worry about this for a while.)

PROTECT YOUR FINANCES

26

GIVE YOUR FINANCES A Y2K TUNE-UP

BACKGROUND

Some experts think there's a high likelihood of turbulent markets and recession in the beginning of the next millennium. Edward Yardeni, chief economist and managing director of the prominent Wall Street investment bank Deutsche Morgan Grenfell, predicts a 40 percent chance of a recession as a direct result of Y2K computer problems. "We must prepare for the likelihood of business failures and the collapse of U.S. government services...there is even the possibility of a depression," says Yardeni.

Key areas of the economy—telecommunications, utilities, and transportation—will have the most difficult time dealing with Y2K. Consumer spending may slow in the second half of 1999 as uncertainty about economic conditions rises and people cut back on purchases. That alone could tip the economy into a recession even if actual Y2K disruptions are minimal. Stock prices could slip as 2000 approaches and investors price in possible Y2K disruptions. It makes no difference whether the disruption actually occurs, mind you. Stocks move on emotion as much as earnings reports.

WHAT YOU CAN DO

It's time to reexamine your investments with an eye toward how they'll be affected if stocks and other investments go down. In the following chapters we'll look at steps you can take to obtain safer investments, making a budget, and getting your credit in order.

Perhaps it's time to cut back your stocks and stock mutual funds in favor of cash and bonds or bond mutual funds. If you want to stay in the stock market, you may want to shift to the most recession-proof stocks, companies with products folks can't do without, such as food, health care, or clothing, for example. In a recession, investors tend to seek out big, well-known companies such as those that make up the Dow Jones Industrial Average or the Standard & Poor's 500. These companies, including Procter & Gamble, Coca-Cola, and RJR Nabisco, tend to have reliable cash flow in good times and bad.

It's a good idea to keep at least three months' take-home pay in safe, liquid investments like insured money market funds, savings bonds, and U.S. Treasuries. (Chapter 27 covers these.)

You may want to consider putting off big purchases until after January 2000, when you'll have had a chance to see which way the economic dice are rolling. You're also more likely to find better bargains in an economic downturn, as businesses slash prices to spur sales.

There's no better time to look at your monthly expenses and cut out frills you probably don't need, like that second telephone line. Recession or no, you'll be financially better off in the long run.

RESOURCES

The Internet is a wonderful source of information about investing and the art of asset allocation, a fancy name for not putting your entire nest egg in one basket.

■ Http://www.money.com, *Money* magazine's Internet site, holds a huge repository of information on nearly every aspect of investing.

■ Http://www.quicken.com, a site run by the popular computer software company, has many basic tools to help you make investment decisions.

■ Http://www.personalwealth.com is run by the venerable ratings company Standard & Poor's and gives access to its entire database on stocks and bonds.

BACKGROUND

If the financial markets turn south because of Y2K, you'll need to shift your money to safer investments until the upset is past. Keep in mind that although safe-harbor investing seems like a great idea all the time, it doesn't work as a long-term strategy. If you invest over a lifetime at rates only 1 to 2 percent better than inflation, you'll have to set aside two or three times as much as the aggressive investor who puts a good portion of his or her assets in the stock market.

The reason is simple. Over the last fifty years, stocks have returned an average 10 percent a year, far outpacing most other investment vehicles. No one knows if stocks will continue to be a good investment, and there will surely be years when your investment declines. With that in mind, here are some safe harbors for your nest egg. (Resources, below, will tell you where to buy these investments.)

By no later than the fall of 1999, consider moving at least one-half of your investments into safer vehicles. If you've already got that much in safer investments, there's no need to do anything. In the first few months of 2000, reexamine the market and rebalance your portfolio if it appears the economy is on track.

WHAT YOU CAN DO

Bank deposits. Everybody knows you can go down to your neighborhood bank and buy a certificate of deposit for terms ranging from a few months to ten years. But you may not know that by shopping nationally for a better rate, you can probably beat your local bank's rate by a full percentage point or more. There's no risk sending a check off to an FDIC-insured bank anywhere in the United States. They're all insured up to $100,000 per account holder.

Short-term bond funds. These are mutual funds that buy top-rated bonds issued by the government and the biggest U.S. corporations. They hold a large basket of these super-safe securities, all of which come due in ninety days or less. This means there's less chance that your principal will fluctuate, though a 1 to 2 percent variation over the course of a year is normal. These funds usually pay about 1 percentage point or so over medium-term CD rates. You can withdraw your money anytime, or write checks against your balance.

Treasury bills and notes. Treasury bills have maturities of three months to one year. These are considered the benchmark safe investment because they're backed by the U.S. Treasury against loss of principal. For longer-term investing you can buy treasury bonds and notes, which mature in ten to thirty years. If you hold these until maturity, your principal will be returned in full as interest is paid along the way. But if you want to cash in early, you may get more or less than your principal, depending on whether there's been any changes in interest rates. Interest rates vary but usually hover around comparable CD rates.

Money markets. These accounts are offered by banks and mutual funds. Bank money market accounts are government insured, mutual funds are not. So you'll get a little more interest with a mutual fund, though neither will pay as well as CD rates. The reason is liquidity: You can take your money out anytime. Rates on these can fluctuate daily.

Savings bonds. These government-insured bonds are sold

in denominations as low as fifty dollars. The bonds are purchased at half their face value; at maturity, which can vary depending on the bond, they pay face value. The rate is based on the yield for U.S. Treasuries. You can defer paying taxes on the interest until the bond is cashed in.

Ginnie Maes. These are issued by a government agency that buys up mortgage notes from consumers. The bonds are guaranteed, and the interest rate is competitive, but there's a catch. If people repay their home loans early, investors in Ginnie Maes get some of their principal back early as well. So you can't be certain of locking in a certain rate for your entire principal for a sustained period of time.

RESOURCES

■ **Bank CDs and money markets.** You can find the best rates on the Internet at www.bankratemonitor.com or monthly in *Money* magazine.

■ **Short-term bond funds.** For phone numbers and current yields on these funds call Morningstar at 312-696-6461 or visit them on the Web at http://www.morningstar.net. Be sure to check the fund's expense ratio; that's the percentage of the fund's assets spent running the fund. The lower this number the better.

■ **Treasuries.** Call 202-874-3000. On the Web go to www.publicdebt.treas.gov.

■ **Money markets.** Check with your local banks. The *Wall Street Journal* lists rates nationwide weekly.

■ **Savings bonds.** These are available at banks. Many employers will allow you to buy savings bonds through payroll deductions.

■ **Ginnie Maes.** These must be purchased from brokers such as Merrill Lynch.

28 | SHAPE UP YOUR CREDIT

BACKGROUND

If Y2K causes a recession and you or your spouse lose your job, it's already too late to do anything about your credit situation. Mistakes on your credit reports, which are common, could keep you from getting the credit you deserve. The old saying about banks only wanting to extend credit to people who don't need it is true. Don't wait until an economic downturn, or a personal calamity like losing your job before checking your credit report. If your credit report is inaccurate, correcting it could take months.

WHAT YOU CAN DO

Now is the time to secure ample credit to see you through if the worst should happen. Credit can be used to see you through hard times, if you line up enough before you have a problem.

Ideally, you want at least three months' living expenses invested in accounts you can get at quickly, and that won't lose their value under any circumstances. In reality, it's hard for many people to put that much aside. But ample available credit is another way to obtain security without scraping together the cash. That simply means lining up credit you can draw on, should the need arise.

A couple of bank credit cards with credit lines equal to three months' expenses may suffice as a cushion. The Resources section below will show you where to obtain credit cards with the best rates. So if your household spends $2,000 a month, you should have at least $6,000 in untapped credit lines. That, or three months' worth of expenses in cash, should see most families through a period of financial difficulty.

Homeowners should consider obtaining a revolving line of home-equity credit. Most banks will charge you the prime rate or a point or so above prime for a home-equity credit line that you can draw on and repay as you please. If you don't use it, the line should cost little or nothing. You can obtain such a credit line at many lenders for a few hundred dollars in closing costs.

Order a copy of your credit report from the three major bureaus listed below. If there are inaccuracies, the bureaus are obliged to investigate and correct them. Do this before you apply for credit.

RESOURCES

■ You can check your credit rating with the three major credit bureaus: Experian, 800-353-0809; Equifax, 800-556-4711; and Trans Union, 800-680-7293. Reports generally cost about eight dollars; they're free if you live in certain states or if you've been turned down for credit, employment, or an apartment in the past sixty days.

■ For information on low-interest-rate credit cards, try CardTrak on the Internet at http://www.cardtrak.com. This free service tracks the rates of hundreds of credit-card issuers and allows you to apply online.

■ *Money* magazine lists low-rate cards each month and at http://www.money.com.

MAKE SURE YOU HAVE AMPLE CASH

BACKGROUND

A cash shortage is a real possibility come New Year's Day 2000 if Americans draw extra cash, fearing that credit cards and cash machines will stop working. If the prospect seems unlikely, consider this: The Federal Reserve, which regulates the nation's money supply, has already announced plans to put an extra $50 billion in circulation as the new year approaches. That's in addition to the $460 billion in U.S. currency already circulating worldwide (60 percent of that circulates outside the United States, so foreigners may well join in any cash rush).

WHAT YOU CAN DO

Don't make the situation worse, but prepare for it. People who live in the snowbelt have seen it happen time and again: Just before a storm, folks clean out the supermarkets, fearing they'll be snowed in. As Year 2000 approaches, and with it the uncertainty of how the computer problem will unfold, people are likely to draw extra cash from banks—lots of it. No one is certain whether bank ATM, check- and card-clearing networks will be fully functional in the new year; thus the need for more cash may be real.

Before you rush down to the bank, some perspective is in order here. Consider just how much cash you would need to conduct your affairs for a few weeks, or even a few months. You'd probably require thousands of dollars. And how would you get the cash to your creditors? The logistics are difficult, to say the least.

Still, you've got to protect yourself. But what if people start lining up at banks and ATMs to get cash? Should you join them?

Well, the Federal Reserve is estimating that each family will take out an extra two weeks' worth of cash before the new year, and adding that amount to the currency supply. So if you take out that much, there should be no shortage.

Just to be on the safe side, however, why not gradually draw out a little extra cash each week in the couple of months leading up to 2000. That way, you won't have to join a line outside the bank, if that does occur.

But before you stockpile wads of currency, remember that you can't collect a dime of interest from cash and you have to safeguard it as well. A cash hoard makes you more susceptible to robbery.

BACKGROUND

With any complex set of numbers the potential for inaccuracy is high. Studies have shown that approximately 5 percent of all loans and mortgages are calculated incorrectly. Y2K computer problems have the potential to introduce a whole new layer of errors into financial calculations.

Most homeowners have mortgage escrow accounts, which are set up by banks to pay your property taxes and insurance. These have an even higher rate of foul-ups. The arrival of 2000, and the fact that 2000 is an out-of-sequence leap year, raises the specter of even greater problems with mortgages, escrow accounts, and home-equity loans.

WHAT YOU CAN DO

There's only one way to tell if your accounts are correct, and that's to check the math. This isn't so hard to do anymore with a number of resources available on the Internet and personal-finance software (see Resources, below). A competent accountant or financial planner can also perform the calculations. For a variable-rate mortgage, make sure they also check whether the rate was figured correctly based on the index that it's tied to (the index will be noted in your mortgage documents).

With the right calculator all you need to do is plug in the numbers to generate a breakdown of how much interest you pay each year, and the outstanding balance on the account. Variable-rate loans are more complicated to check because you must use previous interest rates dating back to when the loan was first started. Your bank may charge a fee to supply this information.

Another thing you can check on your own is your mortgage escrow statement, which by law your bank must mail to you at least once a year. The most common mistake lenders make is holding on to too much of your money.

To check your escrow account, you'll need the month-by-month statement showing the monthly balance and the disbursements from the account over the past year. The lowest monthly balance during the year is the cushion, and that should be no more than two months' worth of escrow payments.

RESOURCES

■ Quicken Deluxe by Intuit is one of the best and most popular PC software programs on the market. It can perform a wide variety of financial tasks, from calculating mortgages to financial planning to bill paying. It's available for Macintosh and Windows PCs for around $50.

■ These two Internet sites are packed with free, easy-to-use financial calculators: http://www.moneyadvisor.com and http://www.timevalue.com.

31 THINK ABOUT GOLD AND SILVER

BACKGROUND

For thousands of years, gold has been portrayed as a safe harbor, a hard asset that can't be devalued. Silver has taken on some of that cachet as well, though its much lower value per ounce means you need a lot of it to hold any real wealth.

At one time, most of the world's currencies, including the dollar, were backed by piles of gold reserves held in central banks. But the currencies of the world have long since been taken off the gold standard and the value of gold has reflected its increasingly unimportant status over the past two decades. After soaring to over $800 an ounce in the inflationary 1970s, gold has been on a steady decline to about $285 late in 1998. There's hardly any period of time in the past twenty years when holding gold would have produced anything but losses. For example, from 1994 to 1997, the price of gold fell by 50 percent.

Now you're probably going to be hearing a lot more about gold as an investment as Y2K approaches. Stocks of gold-mining companies, gold coins, and bullion bars may shoot up in price.

WHAT YOU CAN DO

Gold pays no interest, it's expensive to store safely, and there's a cost to buy and sell it. That said, experts think gold prices could well rise as fear about Y2K escalates. But gold will almost surely head right back down, perhaps even lower than ever, once life returns to normal. So if you buy, be prepared to sell at a moment's notice.

Shares. Stock in gold-mining companies is one way to invest in the metal without having to haul it around. These stocks track the price of gold pretty well. You can buy shares through a stock broker or one of the many low-commission online trading services.

Bullion. You can buy bars of gold in sizes from one ounce to a pound from gold and coin dealers. When you buy you'll generally pay 3 to 5 percent more than the market price, and when you sell, you'll receive about that much less than the market price. The larger the bar, the smaller the markup.

Coins. Gold (and silver) coins have two values—as the metal itself, and numismatic, or collector's, value. A gold coin could be worth many times its bullion value, depending on its condition and scarcity. It's preferable to acquire what is known as scrap or meltdown coins, which are sold by weight, in any condition, and have no numismatic value.

Silver. Much the same rules as gold, except instead of selling for $285 an ounce, like gold, it's less than $5 an ounce. You'd need to obtain two hundred ounces of the stuff just to hold $1,000 worth of value. Coin stores sell bags of pre-1964 U.S. silver coins; in late 1998, $1,000 face value in silver coins sold for about $4,000.

Jewelry. It's probably the worst store of value you can possibly imagine. Jewelry sells as much for its fashion as its metal content, and that can vary from ten karat, which is less than half pure gold, to 24 karat, or pure. You can buy run-of-the-mill jewelry at auctions or from dealers by the gram or ounce.

32 | MAKE SURE YOUR BANK ACCOUNTS ARE SAFE

BACKGROUND

Most large banks have spent lavishly to prevent massive Y2K problems, so much so that even the most pessimistic observers don't envision a meltdown of the banking system come January 3, when banks reopen for business after the new year. Medium-size banks will probably get through without many problems. The small banks will be the ones to watch. The Federal Deposit Insurance Corp. has warned that it might order some banks to shut down and return all deposits to their customers as early as September 1999 if they are not in compliance with federal Y2K standards.

No bank is immune from problems with Y2K, however. Already some debit-card machines at checkout counters have rejected cards with Year 2000 expiration dates. And the potential for inconvenience abounds, such as errors at ATMs, in interest calculations, credit charges, and account balances.

The accounting firm Grant Thornton reports that many small banks aren't taking Y2K seriously enough. Many haven't tested their vaults and other time-sensitive security systems for Year 2000, raising the possibility that they will either be locked out or that doors and vaults will spring open on New Year's Day 2000. Smaller banks rely on computer-dependent outside providers to handle check-clearing and other matters. If outside vendors don't get the problem corrected, these banks will grind to a halt.

WHAT YOU CAN DO

First, don't panic. Your accounts aren't going to disappear. Even if the banking system is brought to its knees by Y2K—and few think this will be the case—each one of your bank accounts is insured up to $100,000 by the Federal Reserve, in essence the U.S. Treasury.

For that reason, don't ever put more than $100,000 in any one bank, not even at different branches of the same bank. Two accounts of up to $100,000 each in the name of each spouse will receive full insurance protection.

To help yourself and the banking system, consider taking a bank holiday. Don't pass or deposit checks in the last week of December and the first week of January, the likely time of maximum strain on the banking system.

If any certificates of deposit or other time accounts come due at that time, make arrangements to roll them over either before or after these crucial weeks. It would be asking for trouble to close on a new mortgage or refinance a loan at this time.

Electronic transfers of money should be avoided as well. If you pay your bills at the end of December or the beginning of January and use electronic payments, you have two choices: Pay electronically and follow up with a telephone call to each creditor a week or so later to make sure they received the proper payment, or pay the old-fashioned way, by mail. But just be sure to send out your bills no later than December 15, so there is plenty of time to process the transaction before Y2K.

Don't fret over direct deposit of your paycheck. It doesn't make sense to stop direct deposit because of the lead time involved to stop and restart such payments, and the relatively small amounts typically involved.

A final word: Try not to conduct any financial transactions during the two crucial weeks, possibly longer, depending on the situation. This includes mutual fund sales and redemptions, stocks and bonds, and annuities. And make doubly sure to keep all bank statements and correspondence, just in case you have to sort out a problem later.

CHECK YOUR INSURANCE POLICIES

33

BACKGROUND

For insurance companies, Y2K is a risk akin to all the hurricanes of the past decade. No one really knows just how much insurers will be asked to pay for Y2K-related damage, but the industry does know this: It didn't factor one dime of these claims into premium calculations. For this reason, the insurers of the world have been furiously backpedaling, contending that policies don't cover losses from an event like Y2K.

The second concern for consumers is whether their coverage is safe. Will your policies be wiped from the bowels of some insurance company's computer? More important, could claims from Y2K overwhelm insurers' ability to pay claims on your life, homeowners, and auto policies? The insurance industry's response to all this has been ostrichlike denial: "We don't believe [Y2K] is an insurance problem," says Steven Goldstein, a spokesman for the Insurance Information Institute, a trade group. On the other hand, the consultants Giga Information Group estimate insurers may pay up to $1 trillion in claims related to Y2K computer problems.

The nature of insurance claims from a never-before event like this is almost impossible to determine. What if the water stops flowing at the stroke of midnight December 31 and your house burns down? What about damage to your property from civil unrest? If the power goes out will your perishable food items be covered? How about claims from traffic accidents if the signals malfunction? Would your policy pay or another policy? Or neither?

WHAT YOU CAN DO

Between now and the end of the year, it's a good idea to read your policies for clues about whether you'll be covered. As renewals occur, take a close look at any literature your insurance companies send you. Older policies, those in force before 1998, will likely contain no mention of Y2K. Those issued in 1998 and later may.

Some insurers have sought to limit Y2K claims to special circumstances; others have excluded them altogether. If that's the case with your homeowners policy, consider shopping around for another insurer that will cover Y2K.

Life policies generally aren't a problem; they'll pay off regardless of the manner of the insured's demise. Auto policies generally cover the car and any liability resulting from its use, but some policies do have exclusions for civil insurrection or damage from "acts of God." Read your policy to find out.

Could your policy be erased by a computer glitch? Yes, but there's not a chance you'll be left uninsured. First, you have your own copies of the policy, and second, insurance companies back up their data in all sorts of ways.

However, the financial stability of an insurance company is an important concern if you're buying a policy for the long haul. You want absolute assurance that a company will be there to pay a claim down the road. Several private companies rate insurers on their ability to pay a claim (see Resources, below).

If any of your current policies were issued by companies with substandard ratings of less than a "B" by a major rating company, consider switching to a company with a top rating.

AM Best and Moody's are two private companies that rate nearly all insurers on their claims-paying ability. Each uses a slightly different rating system, but generally you want to look for companies that are rated "AAA," the best possible rating; "AA," the next best; or "A," a notch down but still in the excellent category. Any insurance company rated in the C's should be avoided.

RESOURCES

■ Most larger libraries carry the rating books of one or the other company. You can also access ratings for free on the Internet at http://www.moodys.com and http://www.ambest.com. There is a charge if you want a full report on an insurance company, but the letter grade should suffice.

■ If you're shopping for a home, auto, or life policy, check out *Consumer Reports*, the monthly magazine published by the nonprofit organization Consumers Union (on the Web at www.consumerreports.org). You'll find ratings and in-depth, unbiased information about buying insurance.

34

BUYING Y2K CLEANUP STOCKS

BACKGROUND

So many companies are making so much money fixing Y2K computer problems that Bloomberg, the financial data provider, started a Year 2000 index back in 1997. By the middle of 1998, the thirty-four stocks in the index had soared more than 50 percent in value. But many of the stocks cooled off in the second half of the year as investors began to worry about whether these companies will fall off a cliff after January 1, 2000, when much of their work will have been completed. That's being called the Year 2001 problem by some financial analysts.

WHAT YOU CAN DO

Stocks in general may be a risky proposition as Y2K takes the stage after so many years in the wings. But there's a good chance that many Y2K specialists will continue to thrive in the 2000s as demand for computer services only continues to increase. You can consider the stocks of companies like Compuware, Keane Inc., Mercury Interactive, and Cognicase, which do Y2K fixes but also market their broader information skills to businesses. Fixing Y2K problems has been a way for these companies and others to get in the door and show their talents.

Stock analysts believe another wave of business for Y2K specialists will occur after January 1, when companies discover computer problems they didn't know they had. Y2K companies with international reach will probably just start to get cracking in 2000 as many businesses overseas clamor for help fixing Y2K problems they couldn't be bothered with—until the symptoms appeared, that is.

If you invest in these stocks, keep in mind that they're highly volatile, capable of soaring 50 percent in a quarter or two, and crashing back down to earth even faster.

RESOURCES

■ A list of stocks in Bloomberg's Y2K index can be found at http://www.bloomberg.com. The Web site has a full menu of personal investing material.

■ The Y2K Investor, at http://www.y2kinvestor.com/intro.html, focuses on Y2K issues as they relate to the financial markets and investing.

35 | FOIL THE Y2K SCAMSTERS

BACKGROUND

Sure as flies are attracted to honey, hoards of fast-buck artists and other assorted crooks are hard at work thinking up ways to use Y2K to separate you from your money. They'll be recycling the tried-and-true scams, but with a Y2K twist.

Already, scamsters have been offering supposedly fail-safe methods to keep your assets safe from an alleged bank meltdown. Crooks dangle promises of super-safe investments or stocks with some Y2K flavor—cash in on the coming disaster, they'll say. Others are touting overpriced property in the mountains, safe from the Y2K mayhem. Says a spokesman for the Federal Trade Commission, "Year 2000 is going to be a field day for the rip-off artists."

WHAT YOU CAN DO

It's easy to say don't fall for this nonsense. But the best scamsters are completely sincere. They mix just enough truth with just enough lies to be believable. They've got impressive-sounding credentials and they know all the buzz words.

Protecting yourself from scamsters boils down to heading off trouble at the pass. Don't take an unsolicited sales calls— from anyone. The minute they start their telephone pitch, say, "I'm sorry, we're not interested," and hang up before the salesperson gets in another word. You may also want to request: "Please put me on your do-not-call list."

Never enter into a transaction with someone who approaches you on the street. Use that same "I'm not interested" line and walk away. Don't give out your credit card or bank account numbers to anyone, even if they say they work for the bank. Any company you deal with already has your account information.

Don't buy anything from people who knock on your door. In fact, don't answer the door if you don't know the person who is knocking.

Identity theft is a growing problem in the United States, and computer malfunctions may create more opportunity for identity thieves to ply their trade. These crooks operate by getting a few key pieces of information about a person, then using these to get still more.

Once the data is compiled, the thieves quickly open as many credit accounts as they can, then drain them with cash advances or purchases. Your Social Security number is one key. Don't give it out to anyone except the government and your employer for tax purposes. The law states that no one else has a right to know your number, yet it's routinely requested. Simply refuse to provide it.

Your driver's license number and checking account number are equally important and should be guarded just as zealously. One way that crooks get checking account numbers is to mail the victim a small rebate check. Once the check is cashed, the crook gets back the canceled check, which has your account number endorsed on the back.

Consider writing to the three credit bureaus (see chapter 28 for contacts) and instruct them to include a note on your file that says: "Do not open credit account without telephoning first." Include your current phone number. This will instruct creditors to call before they open an account in your name.

RESOURCES

■ The National Consumer's League has a special Web site all about scams that allows you to report problems. The National Fraud Information Center is at http://www.nfic.com, or you can call 800-876-7060.

BACKGROUND

The Year 2000 computer bug is likely to affect the U.S. economy and individual companies in complex ways that are impossible to predict. Moreover, Y2K won't occur in a vacuum—all sorts of other factors may come into play, from global market turmoil to interest rates here and abroad to who knows what else.

WHAT YOU CAN DO

Here, in no particular order, are some investments that could benefit from Y2K:

Rare coins. In 1998 and early 1999, demand for investment-grade coins skyrocketed, partly on concern about Y2K. Buying rare coins is less risky nowadays because you don't have to know much about the grading of coins. Two independent coin-grading companies, Professional Coin Grading Service and Numismatic Guaranty Corp., have encased hundreds of thousands of coins in tamper-proof containers with standardized grades. Prices for certified coins are widely available (try http://www.coin-universe.com).

Companies ready for Y2K. As worry among investors about Y2K compliance at individual companies grows, those that have licked their problem are more likely to prosper. These include Aetna, Bankers Trust, AT&T, Cendant, Chase Manhattan, General Motors, McDonald's, Merrill Lynch, Sears, and Xerox. You can find other candidates by following the news. Companies will be announcing their compliance success throughout 1999.

Long-term bonds. These bonds tend to benefit from declining interest rates. And a recession or economic upset would almost certainly cause a decline in interest rates. Zero-coupon bonds are extremely interest-rate sensitive. You can buy long bonds through mutual fund companies like Fidelity and Vanguard or individual bonds from brokers such as Merrill Lynch.

Gold-mining companies. A spike in gold prices seems inevitable. The best way to buy is not the metal, but stock in the gold-mining companies. Some have substantial dividend yields, and reasonable price-to-earnings ratios. Two Wall Street favorites are Barrick Gold and Hecla Mining.

Buying on the dips. Stocks of computer manufacturers, microchip makers, and possibly Internet commerce companies could head south on Y2K fears. Computer makers (Dell, IBM, Compaq) and microchips (Intel, Advanced Micro Devices) may be in for an earnings letdown after the huge increase in orders due to companies replacing their outdated computers for Y2K begins to subside. This may start to show up in stock prices in summer/fall 1999, creating buying opportunities. The stock of Internet commerce companies such as Amazon.com, eBay, and many others could decline if it becomes apparent that sales on the Internet could be disrupted. These are solid companies with good long-term prospects, so a dramatic decline in share price could signal a buying opportunity.

BACKGROUND

If, as some experts say, Y2K kicks off a recession or worse, few jobs will be completely safe. That's why it's important to get your finances in order before there's a problem such as a layoff or cutback in your hours. To start the new century on a firm financial footing, you need to budget. Most people don't like the sound of this—after all, budgets mean discipline and sacrifice, or do they? Not really. Budgets are merely a tool to keep track of what you're spending. Far too many people simply go from month to month writing checks and taking cash from ATMs without giving much thought to where all the money goes. That's the kind of thinking that keeps you from achieving your financial goals. And budgeting will be all the more important if, as some experts believe, the '00s begin with financial turmoil.

WHAT YOU CAN DO

First, tally up your monthly cash flow. Write down your after-tax income for the month, including any money put aside for savings plans, 401(k), and so forth. Next, list your monthly expenses, by type. Include housing, food, car payments, utilities, every single bill you pay. Don't forget the little stuff you pay with cash, such as meals out, the coffee and bagel you buy each morning, kids' lunches, parking, movies.

In separate rows, list any savings plans or money you set aside regularly for mutual funds, the credit union account, and so on. Add separately your spending, savings, and income for the month. While you're at it, multiply each monthly expense by twelve, and you'll see how much you actually spend each year on seemingly small items. Those lunches out are costing you $1,225 a year, aren't they? In ten years, that's enough for a new car, a very nice one if the money was invested aggressively.

Now that you know where the money is going, you can make a budget. The simpler the plan, the better. One way is to take the expenditure amounts you worked up earlier and make an extra column, and perhaps a few more rows near the bottom. The extra column will be headed "spending goal" and that will be your new monthly target for each item.

Many expenses, such as rent or mortgage, are fixed and can't be easily lowered. But look to the marginal items, the little things that add up, for savings. You could cut your cable TV bill by dropping premium channels, or take your lunch to work a few times a week. How about cutting down on packaged junk foods at the supermarket? It's easy to reduce your monthly expenses by 20 percent or more without changing your lifestyle.

Now let's go to the bottom row of your sheet. Add in a row headed "additional savings." That's where you're going to put the money you've cut from your budget. If you've got credit-card bills, the extra money should go toward paying these down each month.

For people with lots of credit-card debt, budgeting can seem hopeless—you just can't get ahead. But consider this: If you're simply making the minimum payments on your credit cards each month, and not adding another penny to the balance, they will never be paid off. The typical card's payment schedule won't erase the balance for twenty years or more—even if you don't add another dime's worth of spending to the tally. Meanwhile, you pay interest on that balance. Once you do pay off a card, cut it up and don't use it anymore. But don't close the account; it's a good idea to have the open credit line to fall back on if times get hard.

You may need to change your spending habits as well. Try to make impulse spending harder by leaving your credit cards and checkbook at home. When you buy something, pay cash. There's nothing like handing over those greenbacks to drive home how much an item really costs.

Any extra money that comes your way should become an excuse to save, not to spend. If you need to purchase big-ticket items such as appliances or furniture, do a reverse credit card. Plan for the expense and set aside a payment each month—in cash if you have to—to cover the amount. Only when you have enough saved should you buy the item.

Couples need to help each other with budgeting, but don't be excessive. Everyone needs a little mad money each month to spend outside the budget. That way budgeting won't take on a prison-ward atmosphere.

RESOURCES

■ If your income isn't enough to cover your bills, and you've got creditors chasing you, it's time to get help. The best place to find this is the nonprofit Consumer Credit Counseling Services. They're listed in the yellow pages of hundreds of cities across the United States. For a small fee, they will help you make a budget and a plan to pay off your creditors. They can stop collection calls and negotiate lower interest rates and payments to fit your budget.

38

WATCH OUT FOR SMALL BUSINESSES

BACKGROUND

Many of the millions of small businesses that serve our needs, from dry cleaning to dental offices to office supplies, aren't getting on the Y2K bandwagon. Survey after survey has shown that these businesses for the most part are going to wing it.

A 1998 study by Wells Fargo Bank showed that 82 percent of small businesses are at risk for Year 2000–related problems. Most exposure comes from computers; a third are at risk from equipment such as cash registers, telephones, or other systems that use time- or date-dependent microchips. The National Federation of Independent Business estimates that more than 330,000 firms may have to close their doors until the problem is fixed and more than 370,000 others could be temporarily crippled by Year 2000 problems.

Many small businesses don't have the resources to track down their computer bugs; they're too busy just trying to stay afloat. That's bad news for millions of Americans, who could be inconvenienced in ways too numerous to imagine.

WHAT YOU CAN DO

If you own a small business, it's not too late to act. A small business has to deal with all the same Year 2000 issues as a large one, except on a smaller scale. Here are some steps you can take.

First, inventory your computer hardware and software and begin an assessment. You can follow the advice in our computer chapters to test and fix your computers. Next, you need to test your other equipment, including cash registers. Most small businesses buy equipment one piece at a time, so don't assume just because one device has no problems the others like it won't either.

Hiring an expert to do this work will likely cost $85 to $100 an hour. Make sure that any specialized software is checked for compliance with the vendor. It's rare that these specialized applications are Y2K compliant. Decide whether to replace or repair equipment that's not compliant.

Many small businesses are apparently figuring they'll purchase all new computer systems, and putting the expense off as long as possible. That's a mistake, because it's going to cost a lot more later. Most small businesses don't have a computer expert and they can't use off-the-shelf software. Throughout 2000 and beyond, computer experts who can set up a new system are going to be so busy with Y2K fixes that you'll have to pay top dollar and perhaps endure a long wait.

Keep in mind that to save money you may be able to upgrade software instead of buying new. Last, you need to check Y2K compliance with your suppliers, vendors, financial institutions, security firms, and anyone else you depend on to keep operating. Just open your checkbook stubs and there's your list to check.

RESOURCES
■ U.S. Small Business Administration (www.sba.gov/y2k) can help small businesses dealing with the Year 2000 problem, including detailed checklists and steps to take.

TRAVEL AND PLAY SAFELY

39

THINK TWICE BEFORE FLYING

BACKGROUND

Few things have been as complicated and vexing for air-travel safety as Y2K. The air-traffic control system is operated by a patchwork of many old computers, some of which date back to the 1960s, and getting these machines ready for Y2K has proven to be a massive task. The airlines themselves must reprogram thousands of computers, both on the planes and on the ground. Over twenty thousand vendors that deliver everything from replacement parts to aviation fuel have Y2K fixes to make.

That's just in the United States and Canada. Worldwide, the problem is much greater. In fall 1998, one-third of eighty-one airports around the world surveyed by the Air Transport Association had made no plans to deal with Y2K.

Only alarmists are suggesting that airplanes will collide or fall out of the sky January 1. Boeing, for its part, says it has identified several hundred of its planes that will need Y2K upgrades and has instructed the airlines that fly them to conduct the repairs.

But given the massive size of the Y2K computer problem, it's surprising how quick the Federal Aviation Administration, which regulates airlines in the United States, has been to deny there could possibly be a risk to passenger safety. The head of the FAA, Jane Garvey, told Congress flatly, "Aviation safety will not be compromised on January 1, 2000, or on any other day."

How can she be so sure? Airports rely on nearby power plants, gas, telephone, and water authorities, all of which are beyond the airports' direct control, and certainly that of the FAA. Officials are so worried that people won't want to fly that Garvey is scheduled to board a flight that will leave the East Coast shortly before midnight on December 31, 1999, and fly west through four continental time zones. Note that she is not planning to fly overseas, however.

WHAT YOU CAN DO

For travel in the United States and Canada around the new year, the chances of anyone's safety being comprised are remote. It wouldn't be overly prudent, though, to avoid domestic air travel from December 31 to, say, January 2.

As for trips to the rest of the world during this critical time period, the best advice is, don't. Says a spokesman for KLM Royal Dutch Airlines: "There might be some areas of the world where you cannot be assured of safety."

Although many people want to celebrate 2000 away from home—and that means air travel—it's still a lousy idea to leave home this New Year's season. There may be other disruptions to deal with on the ground, civil, natural, and man-made.

If overseas travel is unavoidable during this period, fly in and out of the biggest airports you can and only fly on American, Canadian, European, and Japanese carriers. Consider purchasing travel insurance in case your trip is disrupted; this is covered in chapter 41.

RESOURCES

■ The FAA plans to issue warnings if it finds that some places are not safe to visit. The agency has a special Web site at http://www.faa.y2k.com.

■ Another source of up-to-date information can be found at http://www.flightssafety.org. This is a nonprofit site run by a consumer airline safety group.

40 | DRIVE CAREFULLY

BACKGROUND

The Big Three U.S. automakers—Ford, General Motors, and DaimlerChrysler—have given their cars a clean bill of health for Y2K. "We have tested all models, present and past, and there's just nothing in the electronics that would cause a Year 2000 date problem," says Roger Buck, Year 2000 manager for Chrysler Corp.

But all the automakers have Y2K problems in their own factories. GM has been checking 500,000 factory devices, two billion lines of computer code, hundreds of dealerships nationwide, and thousands of suppliers worldwide for Y2K computer bugs.

More of a concern than getting your car started on January 1 is what happens once you hit the road. Power outages could knock out traffic signals. Or, the computer chips that run some signals may malfunction. In Orlando, Florida, for example, the city discovered its central traffic-light computer was clueless when tested with dates beyond December 31, 1999. When the date was rolled over in a test, traffic signals worked in only one mode. Specific programs for rush-hour, holiday, and weekday traffic were wiped out. The potential result had the problem not been fixed could have been gridlock.

Though it's rare for individual older traffic lights to have computer chips or date functions, the systems that synchronize lights in urban areas are run by computers. These could trip up as a result of Y2K glitches.

WHAT YOU CAN DO

If you drive just after December 31, be alert for potential signal outages. Come to a full stop at inoperable lights, even those that are flashing yellow. Slow down and look both ways even when you have the green light.

Slow down on highway stretches where the overhead lighting is not working. Studies have shown these lights greatly increase the driver's field of vision beyond the area where the headlights shine, allowing you to drive safely at highway speeds.

Railroad crossings pose a danger if the signals are not operable. January 1 and after are days to stop and look before you cross any railroad track, because it's impossible to tell whether most railroad signals are functioning correctly or not. When there is no train approaching, such signals are ordinarily blank. Rail officials have stated that some signals and crossings could malfunction due to Y2K computer errors.

Leave extra time for your commute January 3, the Monday after Y2K. That's the day when any Y2K snafus will become apparent to drivers.

BEWARE OF TROUBLE AT SEA

BACKGROUND

It's not a subject you'll read much about in the newspapers, but the shipping industry has got a gigantic Y2K headache. From aging merchant and cruise ships with old computers to coastal authorities, Y2K has been a wake-up call for seafarers.

There's growing concern that locks and canals, including the Panama Canal, may not be operational when the new year begins. Aboard ships, such vital functions as fire-alarm and sprinkler systems, engine management and alarms, radar and navigation, cargo handling and ballast controls, and communications are computer dependent.

So is the infrastructure that supports shipping, from port and cargo operations to shipping-lane traffic management. Maritime experts note that 20 percent of the world's large ships, mostly merchant vessels, won't even be inspected for Y2K problems, creating a potential risk to sea traffic. Chevron has announced it will keep its oil tankers out of restricted waterways, at dock or at sea when 1999 turns to 2000.

The cruise ship industry maintains that it will be ready and cruises will go on as scheduled. On a modern cruise ship there's little chance of personal injury from the sort of Y2K bugs that might affect merchant ships, though you might run into inconveniences. Y2K snafus could include lack of elevator service, skipped ports, downed communications, and the like. This may spoil the fun: Cruise veterans are a demanding lot, and it doesn't take much to start an insurrection.

Don't expect the U.S. government, or any other government, to step in and force Y2K compliance. The world's shipping has long since fled to register in countries like Liberia, known for low taxes and lax regulation.

What You Can Do

The answer to maritime Y2K is simple: Stay off the seas during the crucial time period. If you haven't booked by the time you read this, it's too late to cruise anyway. Agents were reporting nearly full ships for the period. If you've already booked a cruise for the 1999–2000 turnover, bon voyage; it's probably too late to get your money back.

If you do travel by cruise or otherwise in December and January, travel insurance is a necessity. Some travel-insurance plans specifically exclude coverage for anything Y2K related. (Though you should check your policy to be sure, if you've already bought a ticket or plan a cruise at this time.)

These policies cover interruption of your trip, sudden illness, bankruptcy of your tour operators, and more. Such policies cost about $5 per $100 worth of coverage, so insuring a $5,000 trip will cost $250.

One more thing: Beware of documents that relieve the ship's owners of responsibility for any Y2K mishaps or inconvenience. If you are asked to sign such a waiver, you can decline and request a refund. Or if you are intent on going, consider signing and adding this next to your name: "Signed Under Duress."

Resources

■ Your travel agent can help you buy a travel-insurance policy. Or you can call American Express (800-234-0375), Mutual of Omaha's Travel Assure (800-228-9792), or Access America Travel Service Corp. (800-248-8300).

42 BOATERS, TRUCKERS, HIKERS: DON'T GET LOST

BACKGROUND

The Global Positioning System, a network of satellites used to establish navigational positions, has its own end-of-millennium problem. The satellites were put in orbit in the 1970s so the U.S. military could plot any point on the planet with great precision. There are twenty-four satellites in the network and they orbit the earth every twelve hours at a height of approximately twenty thousand kilometers.

Later, the government allowed anybody to use the GPS, and hundreds of products have been developed, from directional systems for automobiles and trucks to handheld devices costing less than $200 that hikers use to find their way through the woods. Many boaters use GPS for navigation, as do the world's airlines.

After August 22, 1999, these devices may become unreliable unless they are updated. It seems the scientists wanted to save computer memory, so they used a time-keeping system that works on a 1,024-week cycle, which ends in the week of August 22, 1999. The length of the cycle, known as an "epoch," was kept at 1,024 weeks because it could be transmitted in a frugal 10-bit block.

Many receivers will be unaffected by the change, but some will suffer a variety of problems, from temporary shutdowns to malfunctions.

WHAT YOU CAN DO

If your boat, truck, or car uses a GPS system, contact the manufacturer about a Y2K software update to fix the problem. Most modern receivers can be easily repaired with a software update. Older receivers may need to be opened up so a new piece of hardware can be installed.

Airliners and large ships have other Y2K problems to deal with, but since none uses GPS as its only navigational system, nobody is worried about them being lost. Small boats do often rely solely on GPS for navigation, so it is imperative that systems on these vessels be examined and repaired.

If you use GPS to hike or boat, be sure to take along old-fashioned compasses and maps just in case the satellite steers you wrong. If you depend only on GPS for navigation in remote areas, obtain and learn how to use standard navigational equipment.

RESOURCES
■ The GPS program has a Web site for Year 2000 preparation activities at http://www.laafb.af.mil/SMC/CZ/homepage/y2000.

DEALING WITH
UNCLE SAM AND THE LAW

DON'T LET THE FEDS FOUL YOU UP

BACKGROUND

The federal government has tens of millions of computers. These are the machines used to keep Social Security checks flowing, to keep track of tax returns, to help administer 1,001 programs and to fulfill literally hundreds of thousands of government duties. Fixing Y2K problems could cost the government about $30 billion, and some agencies are so far behind they'll likely be playing catch-up for many years to come.

The price of disruption could be high. Each week, the federal government sends out $32 billion in Social Security, payroll checks, and other payments. Even a short delay in sending these could be a major shock to the economy.

President Clinton has created a federally controlled Year 2000 Council. Its main role is to assure that federal computers are prepared for the millennium. "The Year 2000 problem is one of the greatest challenges of the Information Age in which we live," Clinton says.

The U.S. House technology panel said in late 1998 that the federal government has not done enough to solve Y2K and must make it "a national priority" to avert a situation that could paralyze government agencies and the economy.

Six government agencies got "F" grades for their lack of preparedness for the so-called Millennium Bug. Those agencies included the Department of Transportation, which oversees the national air-traffic control centers, and the Departments of State,

Energy, and Health and Human Services. The U.S. Environmental Protection Agency and the Agency for International Development also received failing grades. It could be 2005—or later—before all vital government computers at major agencies are fixed if repairs proceed at their 1998 pace.

WHAT YOU CAN DO

The good news is that of twenty-four major federal agencies, four received grades of "A," including the Social Security Administration, the General Services Administration, and the Federal Emergency Management Agency. That means there's very little chance Social Security checks will be delayed, though problems at banks are another story.

Unfortunately, there's not much you can do to help the government along, except making your feelings known to your elected officials. The more political pressure there is to get the job done right and on time, the better chance that will actually happen.

If you have dealings with a government agency, check the Resources section below for sources of current information on that agency's Y2K fixes.

Most important, be sure to keep careful records of any dealings with the government in 1999 and 2000. Send all crucial correspondence by registered mail; make careful notes about who you spoke with and when. Aim to get documents in weeks ahead of the deadline, and follow up with calls and letters to make sure your documents don't fall into a bureaucratic hole.

If you need passports or visas for travel in early 2000, plan to have your documents processed no later than the end of October to be assured of getting them in time. For help dealing with the IRS, see chapter 45.

RESOURCES

■ The Y2K Council has created a Web site at http://www.y2k.gov that provides information on the council and the Year 2000 problem, and lets you search federal sites for more sources.

■ The Centers for Disease Control and Prevention provides a lot of information on Year 2000 implications for public health information at www.cdc.gov/y2k/y2khome.htm.

■ The Federal Deposit Insurance Corp., at www.fdic.gov/about/y2k, provides information on matters related to banking and links to other federal bank regulators' Web sites.

■ The Government Accounting Office, at www.gao.gov/y2kr.htm, provides guides and reports on Y2K plans for all the other government agencies.

BACKGROUND

While all eyes are on the federal government's efforts to deal with Y2K, keep in mind that your local and state governments have even more power to mess up your life. If they don't fix their computers in time, unpleasant things might happen. Your property tax bills may not go out on time or they could be recorded improperly. Your state and local income taxes may be delayed or miscalculated. State highway tollbooths, police Breathalyzer machines, motor vehicle registrations, and licenses could be in jeopardy.

The states realize they're behind in fixing their computers and other devices for Y2K. At least five states—Florida, Georgia, Hawaii, Nevada, and Virginia—have passed laws immunizing state government from lawsuits related to the Y2K bug.

In Massachusetts, for example, in late 1998, more than 40 percent of state agencies had not yet even begun an effort to become Year 2000 compliant. Only about one-third of states began their effort in early 1998, about the time most experts agree there would be a reasonable chance of finishing in time. On the town and city level, the situation varies from gruesome to great depending on where you live.

WHAT YOU CAN DO

You've got to assume that anything can and will go wrong when dealing with your local and state government in 2000. So it's up to you to be prepared. That means carefully keeping all your receipts and paperwork from any dealings with your state, town, or county.

If you pay off a traffic ticket, insist on a receipt and carry it with you when you drive. You wouldn't want a forgetful computer to accuse you of failing to pay or appear in court. That's doubly important for any paperwork you get from the courts. A prudent person would want to secure official copies of any court documents, and perhaps carry certain ones at all times.

Carefully review local tax notices and assessments. Get out your calculator and check the math. Even when everything is functioning normally, it's amazing how many mistakes are made in routine paperwork.

If you're dealing with your state's tax department, try to put off any hearings or sending in paperwork during December 1999 and January 2000. If you do send important documents to your city or state government, use registered mail, return receipt requested. If you have to send time-sensitive items such as tax payments at the end of December or the start of January 2000, hand deliver them if possible, or use an overnight mail service. (Registered mail may take longer to arrive than first-class mail.)

One more thing. Every government in the land has a simple rule about taxes: It doesn't matter if you didn't receive a bill; you owe the tax plus penalty and interest just the same if you're late. So if you don't get a bill, ask for one. It's a good idea to jot down key dates for tax payments in your checkbook ledger as a reminder in case you don't receive a bill.

RESOURCES

■ All the state governments have Internet sites and almost all cover Y2K. To find your state's site simply type the name of your state into the browser address bar, followed by .gov. Example: http://www.massachusetts.gov.

BACKGROUND

A special warning about the IRS: This agency more than any other lives on its paperwork. Computers control the paperwork at the IRS and many of them are outdated, making them prime candidates for Y2K bugs. The General Accounting Office in late 1998 said that it could not accurately predict whether the IRS would be able to fix its computers in time. The agency has got double trouble because it must fix its computer systems to accommodate the Year 2000 and update its software to reflect a host of recent tax law changes.

The agency's record in implementing technology upgrades has been nothing less than abominable. But the IRS commissioner says the agency will be ready for Y2K, though there could be computer glitches in local offices.

WHAT YOU CAN DO

Take special care when sending anything to the IRS in 1999 and 2000. Send your returns and important correspondence by registered or certified mail, return receipt requested. It hardly needs to be said that you must make copies of all documents and store them in a safe place.

If you can, avoid dealing with the agency altogether until it's clear that any computer problems are solved. Request a time extension if you get notice of an audit or other inquiries from the IRS. The agency routinely grants extensions, although if you end up owing additional tax you'll have to pay that much more interest on the amount due to an extension.

Electronic income tax filing, which is growing in popularity, could be affected by computer glitches. If you wait until April 15 to file your return, the IRS's computer problems should be well-known. But you probably don't want to be among the first to file electronically in January or February.

The good news is you'll have a new taxpayer bill of rights in 2000 to protect you from computer foul-ups and unresponsive agents. For example, any correspondence from the IRS must include the name and phone number of an employee that a taxpayer can contact. Under the new law, the burden of proof has been shifted to the IRS in civil-court tax cases if the taxpayer maintained records and met other requirements. It also suspends interest and certain penalties if the IRS failed to notify the taxpayer within eighteen months that taxes were owed. Starting in 2004, the IRS is required to notify the taxpayer within two months.

RESOURCES

■ The Internal Revenue Service, at www.irs.ustreas.gov/prod/news/y2k/, has a list of frequently asked questions about the Year 2000, including what the agency is doing to correct its computers, and how this may affect taxpayers.

GET A Y2K LAW PASSED IN YOUR STATE

46

BACKGROUND

State and local governments have been all too happy to pass legislation that protects them against liability from Y2K computer errors and related foul-ups. Consumers and businesses don't have much protection. Let's say, for example, a computer error made by the government results in foreclosure of your home or business, an incorrect deed being filed, or excess taxes levied. If you live in a state that has shielded itself from liability, you may be out of luck. You'll have to bear the cost of any damage.

However, a handful of states are considering legislation that would give consumers and businesses legal protection against financial liability and damage resulting from certain Y2K computer errors. Such bills would prohibit a home or business from being foreclosed due to a Y2K computer error. It would also prohibit negative entries on credit reports that stem from Y2K foul-ups. The aim of these bills is to temporarily suspend action against a person or business until the error is rectified.

WHAT YOU CAN DO

Ask your state senator and state representative to sponsor a pro-consumer Y2K bill. That's not as hard as it sounds. State legislators are constantly barraged with requests for bills on a thousand different matters by at least as many interest groups. Fact is, when an ordinary citizen comes forward with a well-thought-out bill—with the appropriate legal language—there's a pretty good chance the lawmaker will at least put the bill in the hopper.

Whether they fight actively to get it passed is another matter. In a medium to large state, it's not unusual for several thousand bills to be filed in a legislative season, with perhaps less than fifty making it into law.

The Resources section below will show you where to find what's called "model legislation." This is an all-purpose legal document, usually drafted by a lawyer, that a state can use and adapt for its needs.

You can find the name, address, and phone number of your state legislators in the telephone book. Look in the blue pages, or government section. You can copy the model bill from the Internet and send it along with a note of support. A phone call is even better. If you aren't able to talk to your elected official, ask for his or her legislative assistant.

RESOURCES

■ The Cassandra Project, at http://www.cassandraproject.org/ home.html, has the model bill online. Or you can write to: The Cassandra Project, PO Box 8, Louisville, CO 80027. The phone is 303-664-5227.

KEEPING UP TO DATE

47 | READ UP ON Y2K

Of the flood of Y2K books on the market, this list includes the top sellers. For an up-to-date list of titles, use the search engines of online booksellers such as http://www.amazon.com and http://www.barnesandnoble.com.

Awakening: The Upside of Y2K by Judy Laddon, Tom Atlee, and Larry Shook (The Printed Word, $10.00) is about the human side of Y2K, on connecting with what's really important in our lives. The focus is on nurturing a new world that's more healing, compassionate, sustainable, and fun.

Time Bomb 2000: What the Year 2000 Computer Crisis Means to You! by Edward Yourdon and Jennifer Yourdon (Yourdon Press Computing Series, $19.95) includes writings on the Y2K problem and presents a collection of scenarios ranging from the best we can hope for to the worst cases.

Year 2000 Solutions for Dummies by Kelly C. Bourne (IDG Books Worldwide, $24.99) explains why this problem is going to occur, what types of computers will be affected, and where to start to fix them.

The Year 2000 Legal Handbook by Howard A. Gutman (Year 2000 Publishing Co., $145.00) is a detailed study of Year 2000 legal issues written in an understandable fashion.

The Millennium: A Rough Guide to the Year 2000 by Nick Hanna (Rough Guides, $8.95) includes everything readers need to know about the coming millennium—celebrations and parties, pilgrimages and festivals, millennium projects, and more.

Countdown Y2K: Business Survival Planning for the Year 2000 by Peter de Jager and Richard Bergeon (John Wiley & Sons, $29.99).

Finding and Fixing Your Year 2000 Problem: A Guide for Small Businesses and Organizations by Jesse Feiler and Barbara Butler (Academic Press, $39.99).

Year 2000 in a Nutshell: A Desktop Quick Reference by Norman Shakespeare et al. (O'Reilly & Associates, $19.99).

The Millennium Bug: How to Survive the Coming Chaos by Michael S. Hyatt (Regnery Press, $25) asks, How bad could Y2K get? Find out with this rather alarmist account.

The World Wide Web is an excellent source of up-to-date information on Year 2000 issues. Just keep in mind that the Web is a vast repository, but not in the same way as a library. Anybody can put things on the Internet, true, false, high quality, or no quality at all. So always consider the source of the material. The sites listed below are among the most popular on the subject, though some of them tend to take a somewhat alarmist view of the problem.

The following are the top Web sites:

Ed Yardeni's Y2K Reporter, http://www.yardeni.com cyber.html. Mr. Yardeni is a top economist for Deutsche Bank, one of the world's largest financial institutions. His site has links and gives lots of advice about dealing with Y2K. You can read his testimony before Congress here as well.

Gary North's Y2K, http://www.garynorth.com. A well-presented view of Y2K from many angles, though a bit alarmist.

The Cassandra Project, http://www.cassandraproject.org. A fascinating site that's geared toward increasing public awareness about Y2K.

Year 2000 Information Center, http://www.year2000.com. The site is run by Peter de Jager, who has attempted to post every Year 2000 story on the Web.

Y2K Help!, http://www.y2k.comco.org/index.htm. Solutions for Year 2000 compliance problems. A commercial site with articles, links, and compliance statements.

Year 2000 Status, http://www.y2k-status.org/. This site

offers status reports on the world's progress to eliminate or alleviate the Year 2000 problem. Links to many Y2K resources.

Year2000.com Law Center, http:www.//year2000.com. Focuses on the legal, accounting, and insurance aspects of the Year 2000 problem.

The Y2K Investor, http://www.y2kinvestor.com. Y2K-related investment information.

Y2K Stuff, http://www.y2kstuff.com. Shows you where to buy all sorts of items related to Y2K, from T-shirts to computer programs.

Y2K Times, http//www.y2ktimes. A rich source of papers, articles, reviews, and links.

President's Council on Year 2000 Conversion, http://www. y2k.gov/; 888-872-4925. The toll-free service is in operation from 9 A.M. to 8 P.M. EST. It is staffed by employees of the General Services Administration's Federal Information Center and will connect citizens to prerecorded information about the computer bug as well as to information specialists who can answer questions.

49 | JOIN A Y2K GROUP

BACKGROUND

Hundreds of informal groups meet to plan for and discuss Y2K issues that affect their community. Many of these groups share information on solving Y2K problems. For example, in Norfolk, Nebraska, a town meeting sponsored by the town council, the local community college, businesses, and a public TV station drew two hundred people to focus on the effects of Y2K. More than 120 signed up for groups to tackle such projects as how the local schools and the economic development plan will be affected. The group wants to make sure that schools are equipped to provide water, food, cooking, and a warm space through the winter. Local business people were able to help each other in solving their Y2K problems.

WHAT YOU CAN DO

You can join a group anywhere simply by getting on their e-mail list. Or find a local chapter; many of them hold regular meetings to exchange ideas. The list that follows is for the United States. You can obtain updates of this information at the nonprofit Cassandra Project's Web site at http://www.cassandraproject. org/home.html.

If you'd like to send and receive e-mail but you don't have a computer or online account, here's what to do: Go to your local library and ask to use the Internet. Once you get on, type http://www.hotmail.com into the browser. There, you'll find instructions on how to open a free e-mail account that will provide you with a secure way to send and receive messages.

Alabama

Birmingham Y2K Community Preparedness Group,
Birmingham, AL. Contact: Tracy. E-mail:
bhamy2k@aol.com.

North Alabama Y2K Community Action Group, Huntsville,
AL. Contact: Kellie Andrews. E-mail:
andrewsk@nichols.com.

Alaska

The Tides of Change, Juneau, AK. Contact: David La
Chapelle, PO Box 21592, Juneau, AK 99802. E-mail:
dlachape@ptialaska.net.

Alaskans for Y2K Awareness, Douglas Island, AK. Contact:
Chris Dolmar or Jeff Long. E-mail: dolmar@ptialaska.net.

Arizona

Timberline, Flagstaff AZ. Contact: Steve Haag. E-mail:
shaag7@aol.com.

Tucson Year 2000 Center, Tucson, AZ. Contact: Thomas
Greco, 520-792-6438. E-mail: circ@azstarnet.com.

Y2K Coalition, Prescott, AZ. Contact: Will Hepburn or Erin
Mitchell, 520-778-4000. E-Mail:
y2kcoalition@hotmail.com.

Phoenix Y2K City Action Counsel, Phoenix, AZ. Contact:
David Bradshaw, 800-289-2646. E-mail:
ideaman@y2knet.com.

Concerned Christians for Christ Preparedness Group,
Prescott, AZ. Contact: Greg Wiatt, 520-541-9727.
E-mail: gwiatt@northlink.com.

New Heaven New Earth, Sedona, AZ. Contact: David
Sunfellow. E-mail: nhne@sedona.net.

Y2K Community Preparedness Group, Tucson, AZ. Contact: Laurence J. Victor, 520-319-1873. E-mail: nuu@azstar-net.com.

Arizona R.V. Y2K Community, Sedona, AZ. Contact: Jim, 520-204-2837. E-Mail: Jimreese@kacina.net.

Y2K Good Sam Christian Neighbors, Cottonwood, AZ. Contact: Carroll "Doc" Carruth, 520-639-3548. E-mail: cdcarruth@cybertrails.com.

Arkansas

NW Ark Y2K Community Prepare, Northwest, AR. E-mail: acts14@juno.com.

California

East Bay Y2K Prep Group, Concord, CA. Contact: Dan Leahy. E-mail: danleahy@primenet.com.

Santa Barbara 2K-wise, Santa Barbara, CA. Contact: Mark. E-mail: sb2kwise@silcom.com.

Christian Family Y2K Preparedness Group, Sunland, CA. Contact: Gene and Juanita Hanna. E-mail: Jdida@aol.com

Santa Cruz County Y2K Preparedness Committee, Santa Cruz, CA. Contact: Mihacla Moussou. E-mail: mihaela@co-i-l.com.

Metro Church Y2K Task Force, Santa Monica, CA. E-mail: rex@losthorizon.com.

Marin Y2K Action, San Rafael, CA. Contact: Wendy Tanowitz. E-mail: wendyt@jps.net.

Year 2000 Action Group, Chico, CA. Contact: John O'Brien, PO Box 1591, Chico, CA 95927-1591. E-mail: nein99@hotmail.com.

South Bay Y2K, Los Angeles, CA. Contact: Alain Durocher or Elle D'Coda. E-mail: alain@wonderlan.com or dcoda@therapist.net.

Napa Valley Y2K, Napa Valley, CA. Contact: Mick Winter, 707-257-2737. E-mail: mick@westsong.com.

North Santa Barbara County Y2K Preparedness Group, Orcutt, CA. Contact: Bill Seavey, PO Box 2916, Orcutt, CA 93457; 805-938-1396. E-mail: wlseavey@hotmail.com.

Colorado

Roxborough Park Community Readiness 2000 Team, Roxborough Park, CO. Contact: John N. Miller, 303-933-4761. E-mail: jnmiller@uswest.net.

Franktown Community Preparedness Group, Franktown, CO. Contact: Cindy Brown. E-mail: cindy@forklift-specialists.com.

Volunteer Citizens of Arapahoe County, Arapahoe County, CO. Contact: Jim Stanton. E-mail: taur696@aol.com.

Loveland 2000, Loveland, CO. Contact: Steve Teichner, director, 970-663-2998. E-mail: Loveland2K@aol.com.

Boulder County Y2K Community Preparedness Group, Boulder, CO. Contact: John Steiner. E-mail: JASteiner@aol.com.

Fort Collins Year 2000 Support, Fort Collins, CO. Contact: Jeff Hogan, 970-484-9179. E-mail: jeffhogan@juno.com.

Connecticut

Westport, CT., Selectman's Year 2000 Committee, Westport, CT. Contact: Ed Perrault, 203-222-8675. E-mail: EdPerrault@compuserve.com.

District of Columbia

Friendship Heights Year 2000 Group, Washington, DC.
Contact: Stephen Balkam. E-mail: sbalkam@rsac.org.

Florida

Y2K for Common Folk, St. Augustine, FL. Contact: Anne T.
Sargent, 904-794-2040. E-mail: Spiritwman@aol.com.

Community Y2K Planning Guide, Pensacola, FL. Contact:
Blane Land, 850-484-9940. E-mail: blane@aloha.net
Suncoast.

Community Institute of Noetic Sciences (SCIONS), Tampa
Bay, FL. Contact: Sharon Joy Kleitsch, 727-550-9660.
E-mail: kleitsch@gte.net.

Y2K/The prudent foresee & prepare—Prov. 22:3, Plantation,
FL. Contact: Lolita. E-mail: transetcet@aol.com.

First Baptist Church of SouthWest Broward, Hollywood, FL.
Contact: Ken Griesbach. E-mail: tentmaking@juno.com.

Pinellas County Grassroot Effort, Pinellas County, FL.
Contact: Arthur Bouchard. E-mail: abouchar@gte.net.

Citizens for a Stable Community, Clearwater, FL. Contact:
James Hadley, 727-447-2147. E-mail: citstacom@earth-
link.net.

Georgia

Y2K Contingency and Awareness Group—Newton County,
Georgia, Covington, GA. Contact: Susan Mills. E-mail:
newtoncoy2k-subscribe@egroups.com.

Rainy Day Supply, Cedartown, GA. Contact: Tom or Sharon
Miller, PO Box 1901, Cedartown, GA 30125. E-mail:
rdsupply@bellsouth.net.

Y2K Group, Marietta, GA. Contact: Sheila Lewis Busby,

770-333-0448. E-mail: sheila@lookup.org.

Douglasville Community Y2K, Douglasville, GA. Contact:
Mary Kochan. E-mail: mkochan@mindspring.com.

Y2K Group, Atlanta, GA. Contact: Jim Greer, 770-992-
9709. E-mail: jmgreer@accessatlanta.com.

Omega Group, Savannah, GA. Contact: Bill Lynes, 912-897-
5153. E-mail: wlynes@g-net.net.

Hawaii

Spirit of Truth Ministry, Kaneohe, HI. Contact: Mark
Miyashiro, PO Box 5344, Kaneohe, HI 96744; 808-236-
1372. E-mail: Alohamin@aol.com.

Share a Rainbow, Lihue, Kauai, HI. Contact: Jo B., 808-246-
6085. E-mail: greydog@aloha.net.

Kauai Community Self Reliance Cooperative, Kauai, HI.
Contact: Karlos deTreaux. E-mail: Y2K@aloha.net.

Illinois

Y2K & Beyond, Golconda, IL. Contact: Ron Dunning. 618-
949-3798. E-mail: tronone@shawneelink.com.

Children of Liberty, Chicago, IL. Contact: Antoine Denerome.
E-mail: ThohT@yahoo.com.

Indiana

Y2K Indianapolis, Indianapolis, IN. Contact: Kent Morgan,
317-897-1320. E-mail: smorgan@on-net.net.

Indianapolis Y2K Awareness Project, Indianapolis, IN.
Contact: Mark Magers. E-mail: magers@gateway.net.

Indiana Y2K Preparedness Project, Mishawaka, IN. Contact:
Cindy Jacobs, PO Box 6735, Mishawaka, IN 46660.
E-mail: cjac@michianatoday.com.

Kansas

Western KS. Y2K Group, Pratt, Kingman, Medicine Lodge,
KS. Contact: Kylie Moyers, 316-246-5383. E-mail:
nicole7@rocketmail.com.

Kentucky

Mason County Personal Preparedness Group, Maysville, KY.
Contact: John Price. E-mail: qemaster@rocketmail.com.

Louisiana

Shreveport-Bossier Y2K Awareness Group, Shreveport, LA.
Contact: Ronnie Free. E-mail: freesinc@softdisk.com.
Acadiana Y2K Awareness Group, Lafayette, LA. Contact:
David M. Goodwyn, 318-896-7092. E-mail:
dgoodwyn@acadianay2k.org Belividere.

Maryland

Y2K Wise, Anne Arundel County, MD. Contact: Eileen or
Patti. E-mail: y2kwise@bigfoot.com.
Southern Maryland Millennium Action Committee, Charles,
Calvert, St. Mary's counties, MD. Contact: James
Crawford, 301-274-4747. E-mail: smmac@us2000.org.

Massachusetts

Neighborhood Association Year 2000 Project, Lowell, MA.
Contact: Ian Wells, 978-446-0114. E-mail: ianwells@big-
foot.com.

Michigan

Y2K, Leland, MI. Contact: Andrew McFarlane, 616-256-
2829. E-mail: l2k@leelanau.com.

Paint Creek Reserves, Rochester, MI. Contact: Lee Knudsen, PO Box 82027, Rochester, MI 48308. E-mail: Featheredhook@msn.com.

Year 2000 Citizen Action Group, Oakland County, MI. Contact: Bob Mangus, 810-912-8729. E-mail: rmangus@netquest.com.

Minnesota

Mpls/St. Paul Y2K Preparedness Group, Minneapolis, St. Paul, MN. Contact: Nate, 612-537-5298.

Mississippi

The Heavenly Way Adventistry, Rienzi, MS. Contact: Walter McGill, 601-462-7552. E-mail: crmin@ix. netcom.com.

Missouri

Mid-Missouri Y2K Project, MO. Contact: F. Williams. E-mail: fwilliams@trib.net.

Salt & Light in 2000, New Haven, MO. Contact: Chris Baker. E-mail: ckbaker@fidnet.com.

Nevada

Las Vegas Y2K Community Preparedness Group, Las Vegas, NV. Contact: Amanda Walker. E-mail: arwalker@earth-link.com.

New Jersey

East Brunswick Area Y2K Community Preparedness Group, East Brunswick, NJ. Contact: James Ranish, 732-417-7308. E-mail: y2kok@aol.com.

Atlantic County Y2K Action!, Margate, NJ. Contact: Glenn
   L. Klotz. E-mail: lee00@earthlink.net.

New Mexico
Northern New Mexico Y2K, Los Alamos, NM. Contact: John
   Zoltai, 505-672-3177 E-mail: jtz@lanl.gov.
The Millennium Group, Albuquerque, NM. Contact:
   Timothy Holmes, 505-332-0353. E-mail:
   timothy@swcp.com.
East Mountain Y2K, Tijeras, NM. Contact: Wade Douglas,
   PO Box 1450, Tijeras, NM 87059. E-mail:
   skygazer@rt66.com.

New York
Tri-State Year 2000 Overcomers, New York City and suburbs
   (NJ, CT). Contact: Bob Ellis, 914-682-1859. E-mail:
   EllisB@conedsolutions.com.
Corning Care Givers, Corning, NY. Contact: Joyce Jagger,
   607-936-4389. E-mail: jaguar244@aol.com.
Ad-Hoc Emergency Preparedness Y2K Group, Tompkins
   County, Ithaca, NY. Contact: Gene Ira Katz or Hope
   Bitzer, PO Box 6601, Ithaca, NY 14851. E-mail:
   geneirakatz@yahoo.com.
Millenium Awareness Group, Sloatsburg, NY. Contact: Brian
   Donnelly, 914-753-9039. E-mail: docveneer@yahoo.com.

North Carolina
The Old Ways, Charlotte, NC. Contact: Dan and Nora
   Waltman, 704-545-8780. E-mail: CNDETECT@aol.com.
Fayetteville Y2K, Fayetteville, NC. E-mail: jonsarah-
   goebel@mindspring.com.

Earthgarden Sustainable Living Community, Asheville, Greensboro, NC. Contact: Carolyn Deal, 336-854-4555. E-mail: cwdeal@aol.com.

Ohio

The Trib Force, Harrison, OH. Contact: Rick McKinney, 812-637-1918. E-mail: JwalkerRMc@aol.com.

Christ is our Sufficiency, Highland County, OH. Contact: Mark and Debbie Peters, 937-927-5684. E-mail: judah7@bright.net.

Oregon

Polk Y2K Taskforce, Dallas, OR. Contact: Steve Bennett. E-mail: polky2k@navicom.com.

Eugene Y2K Ready User's Group, Eugene, OR. Contact: Cynthia Beal. E-mail: cabeal@efn.org.

Rogue Valley Year 2000 (RV-Y2K) Task Force, Medford, OR. Contact: 541-608-9265. E-mail: countdown@rv-y2k.org.

Pennsylvania

DelCo Y2K Awareness, Aston, Delaware County, PA. Contact: Robb Ware. E-mail: Y2KROBB@aol.com.

Health & Wellness, Green Lane, PA. Contact: Carolyn. E-mail: HealthAndWellness@msn.com.

Beaver County Y2K Community Preparedness Group, Beaver County, PA. Contact: Susan K. Minarik, 724-847-9575. E-mail: sminarik@ccia.com.

Tennessee

Y2K and Beyond, Franklin, TN. Contact: Jerry Walkoviak. E-mail: signsofthetime@compuserve.com.

Tri-Cities 2000, Johnson City, Bristol, Kingsport, TN. Contact: Elizabeth Obos, 423-434-2172. E-mail: jlw@planetc.com.

The Waller Group, Nashville, TN. Contact: Craig Waller, 615-356-7624. E-mail: buznethel@mindspring.com.

Texas

Wings of Eagle, San Antonio, TX. Contact: Elia G. Pardo. E-mail: cgjesu9@aol.com.

Kingsland Community Fellowship, Northeast TX. Contact: Rev. Michael Rothman, 903-791-1246. E-mail: acts14@juno.com.

Tyler 2000 Prep, Tyler, TX. Contact: R.K. Mount. E-mail: rkmount@t2kprep.com.

Year 2000—Texarkana in Action, Texarkana, TX. Contact: Lisa Zach, 903-792-7448. E-mail: lzach1@gte.net.

Austin Community Emergency Preparedness Group, Austin, TX. Contact: Sam Loy, 512-282-6053. E-mail: sloy@iphase.com.

Y2K Alert Group, Austin, TX. Contact: Richard Lanoue, 512-833-9198. E-mail: idrive4free@yahoo.com.

People Aglow Ministry, Houston, TX. Contact: Lamesia A. Holiday. E-mail: peopleaglowministry@prodigy.net.

Permian Basin Community Preparedness, Midland-Odessa, TX. Contact: Tom White, 915-367-4446. E-mail: tom.w@usa.net.

Texas Statewide Y2K Preparedness, Montgomery County and other counties, TX. Contact: Adrian D. Heath, 281-292-4889. E-mail: adheath@swbell.net.

Utah

Y2k User's Group, Salt Lake City, UT. Contact: John Horton 801-240-2341. E-mail: hortonjl@ldschurch.org.

Provo/Orem Y2K Preparedness Group, Provo, UT. Contact: Russell Peterson. E-mail: ProvoY2K@yahoo.com.

Northern Utah Y2K Community Preparedness Group, Ogden, UT. Contact: Jennifer Mueser Bunker, 801-782-1942. E-mail: WarmCreeks@aol.com.

Vermont

N.H.-VT. Committees of Correspondence, Bradford, VT. E-mail: concomm@usa.net.

Virginia

Simple Abundance, Abingdon, VA. Contact: Tony McKenna. E-mail: free@naxs.com.

Middle Peninsula Y2K Preparedness Network, Gloucester, VA. Contact: Mark, 800-416-2879. E-mail: ymmarket@inna.net.

Northern Virginia Year 2000 Community Preparedness Group, Fairfax, VA. Contact: Tonja Bento. E-mail: jbento@erols.com.

Springfield Year 2000 Community Preparedness Work Group, Springfield, VA. Contact: Jay Golter, 703-971-8641. E-mail: JGolter@aol.com.

West Virginia Year 2000 Preparedness Group, Springfield, VA. Contact: Warren Brock, 304-736-2699. E-mail: lon1937@aol.com.

Washington

Jefferson County Y2K Action Group, Port Townsend, WA. Contact: Matt Ready, 360-385-5598. E-mail: y2k@olympus.net.

Year 2000 Preparedness Council, Seattle, WA. Contact: Anita Kulp. E-mail: Year2KPrep@aol.com.

Wyoming

Y2K Remnant, Buffalo, WY. Contact: Jeff Martin. E-mail: Shadetree1@hotmail.com.

THE LAST WORD

50 | SIMPLIFY YOUR LIFE

BACKGROUND

Thanks to the Y2K computer bug, the twenty-first century will probably get off to a rocky start. Whatever inconveniences—or even disasters—occur, some people may rue that day that computers and their microchips became such an integral part of our lives. That's too bad, because on the whole the microchip has brought profound change for the better to the lives of almost every American. And the Y2K error is the fault of man, not computers. As long ago as 1984, computer experts were warning about the problem, but no one in charge was listening.

Our automobiles run trouble free for 100,000 miles or more without so much as an adjustment, thanks to the microchip. Countless microchips embedded in the innards of everything from televisions to airplanes to wristwatches have helped build a new age of information access and convenience. In the field of medicine, devices such as laser eye surgery have literally helped thousands to see again.

To be sure, there's a downside to the microchip. It has created greater and greater demand for the world's limited resources, two-fifths of which the United States continues to use each year. A culture of waste and indifference has been fostered by a throw-away attitude and a voracious appetite for consumer goods, quickly cast aside for the next bauble. Far too many people have hocked themselves into debt to obtain the trifles of the electronic age.

So when our circuitry turns against us, we're resentful. But few will bother to make their lifestyle more sustainable. It's not so hard to do, and you may be surprised how much satisfaction can be derived from simplicity.

WHAT YOU CAN DO

Ten ways to simplify your life:

1. Stop directing your goals toward the acquisition of more and more consumer goods. Before you buy another appliance, the latest model, the newest fad, ask yourself these questions: Do I really need this? Will it make my life better? Will I devote more than just a few moments to using this before it's shuffled off to molder somewhere?

2. Buy used instead of new. Perfectly good used items are the biggest bargain around. Take computers, for example. A nice model a year or two old can be purchased for a few hundred dollars, compared to $1,000 or more for a new one. Fact is, few people need the power of the new ones anyway. And not one bit of the earth's resources are consumed when you buy used. Another example: Used cars not more than a year or two old cost a third less than a new car and will run dependably just as long, for all practical purposes.

3. When you do buy new, go for simplicity. Most consumer goods are loaded with features that people don't need. These features drive up the cost of the product enormously. Think of the last time, for example, you changed the settings on your dishwasher, or used your VCR's fancy programming features.

4. Use up the goods you do have. Drive that car until the wheels fall off. You'll get the lowest cost per mile, and you'll keep down the number of new cars that are manufactured each year. The same advice holds for appliances, clothes, all sorts of items. People throw out perfectly good things all the time to

make way for new shiny ones that do exactly the same thing.

5. If you must get rid of serviceable goods, don't take them to the dump. Recycle by donating them to charitable groups, who will see they are put back into service.

6. Cut down your waste. Recycle newspapers, plastic, and paper if you're not doing so already. Start a compost pile if you've got a bit of land available.

7. Think smaller. The average new American house has grown by 40 percent since 1970. Three and four bathrooms are common these days, as are huge rooms with high, expensive-to-heat ceilings. It's time that we started questioning this edifice complex. Smaller cars would also have a huge effect on the environment. But Americans have fallen in love with gas-guzzling, unwieldy sport-utility vehicles, an obsession that has brought the average gas mileage of the U.S. fleet back to where it was in the early 1970s.

8. Set an economical example for your children. By acting with conservation in mind, you lead them with your deeds. Trying to fulfill your child's every material desire sends two wrong messages: that all is easily attainable, and that baubles are worth having even if you can afford them.

9. Cut down your driving and shuttling your kids around. You'll not only save gas, you'll save wear and tear on yourself and your family.

10. Make a difference in your community. Pitch in on projects that serve everyone, and encourage your children to do the same.

ABOUT THE AUTHOR

WILLIAM D. McGUIRE is a widely published journalist with a special interest and expertise in millennium issues. He spent nine years as a writer and editor at *Consumer Reports*, where he specialized in personal finance and technology, and he is currently editor of Money.com, the Web site of *Money* magazine. His work has received regional and national awards.